· T R O P H I E S ·

Language Handbook

Grade 5

Printed in the United States of America

ISBN 0-15-325067-4

10 073 10 09 08 07 06 05

Orlando Boston Dallas Chicago San Diego

Visit *The Learning Site!*
www.harcourtschool.com

CONTENTS

Visit *The Learning Site!*
www.harcourtschool.com

Contents

Contents

contents

Your Best Writing

Writing is communicating. Good writing is communicating well. It's as simple—and as tricky—as that! Your best writing should communicate as effectively as your best speaking. When you become comfortable with writing, it becomes almost as easy as talking to a friend. However, it takes practice to become comfortable with the act of writing. That's where the *Language Handbook* comes in.

This handbook will give you the skills, strategies, tips, and models you need to become a relaxed, confident writer. Let's begin with an overview of the writing process and some useful strategies.

The Writing Process

No matter how confident you are, your best writing may not come from your first attempt. Even professional writers don't often get it right the first time. They review, revise, throw out ideas, and think up new ones. Although no two people work in exactly the same way, most writers do go through the following five stages.

Prewriting

In prewriting, you plan what you are going to write. You choose a topic, identify your audience and purpose, brainstorm ideas, and organize information.

Drafting

In this stage, you refer to your prewriting plan and express your ideas in sentences and paragraphs.

Revising

This stage marks the beginning of the editing process. You may ask others for input or reread your work yourself. Make any changes that improve your writing and help you communicate better.

Proofreading

This stage completes the editing process. You check for errors in grammar, spelling, capitalization, and punctuation. Then make a clean, final copy of your composition.

Publishing

Finally, you communicate with your audience by choosing a way to share your work. You may present your work orally, add pictures or diagrams and display your work, mail a letter, or make a book.

Keeping a Writer's Journal

Writers of all ages keep journals. In a journal, you can jot down ideas for writing. You can reflect on things you see or learn, take notes on events or issues, and try out different forms of writing.

Start your own journal by choosing a notebook you like. Decorate it if you wish. Then begin to fill the pages with your ideas and writing experiments.

At the back of your journal, you may wish to keep a **Word Bank** of vocabulary that you can use in your writing. Write down interesting words and expressions that you hear or read. Put your words into groups, such as sports words, words naming feelings, strong verbs, and vivid adjectives.

Keeping a Portfolio

A portfolio is a collection of work. Artists and architects keep portfolios of their sketches and completed designs. They show them to people who are interested in their work. Writers can keep portfolios, too.

It's often useful to keep two kinds of portfolios. You can put your works-in-progress or unfinished ideas into a **working portfolio**. Your finished writing can go into a **show portfolio** to be shown to others. As you complete projects in the working portfolio, you can move them to the show portfolio.

You may use either kind of portfolio in writing conferences with your teacher. In your writing conference, discuss your accomplishments. Tell what is easy and hard for you about writing. Decide how you can improve, and set goals for yourself as a writer.

Reading ↔ Writing Connection

Reading can help you become a better writer. As you read newspaper articles, magazine ads, stories, and letters, read actively. Think about the purposes of different kinds of writing. Decide whether the writer makes ideas clear and interesting.

Writer's Craft and Writing Traits

In the dictionary, *craft* is defined as "skill in doing or making something." To a writer, craft is the strategies and skills needed to communicate ideas well. Like cabinetmakers or weavers, writers must practice their skills. Daily practice is the key to becoming a better writer.

Good craftspeople also understand and appreciate their material. Painters learn to use paints, brushes, and canvas. Weavers work with yarn or thread. Writers work with words.

Writers learn to work with words by studying the qualities, or traits, of good writing. You will learn more about these traits as you read this handbook.

The Traits of Good Writing

Conventions
Correct punctuation, grammar, spelling

Organization
Logical and clear structure

Development
Reasons and details

Word Choice
Vivid verbs, strong adjectives, specific nouns

Focus/Ideas
Interesting, clear content

Voice
Viewpoint and tone

Effective Paragraphs
Similar ideas grouped together

Effective Sentences
Flow, rhythm, variety

Traits Checklist

As you practice your craft daily, use these questions to focus your thinking. When you can answer most of them with a "yes," you know you are becoming skilled at your craft. The lessons in this handbook will help you work on those areas that still need improvement.

☑ **FOCUS/IDEAS**	Do I stick to the topic? Do I keep my purpose and audience in mind?
☑ **ORGANIZATION**	Do I have a clear beginning, middle, and ending?
☑ **DEVELOPMENT**	Are my ideas supported with details and reasons?
☑ **VOICE**	Is my voice strong? Could a reader easily understand my feelings about the topic?
☑ **EFFECTIVE SENTENCES**	Are my sentences clear? Do I use different sentence types?
☑ **EFFECTIVE PARAGRAPHS**	Are similar ideas grouped together in paragraphs? Do I use transitions to connect ideas?
☑ **WORD CHOICE**	Do I use exact and vivid nouns, verbs, and describing words?
☑ **CONVENTIONS**	Are my punctuation, grammar, and spelling correct?

Try This! Choose a piece of writing that you recently completed. Read it against the Checklist above. What did you do best? Which areas need improvement? Make some changes in your writing if you wish.

Focus/Ideas

Did you ever tell stories when you were a little child? You probably had plenty of ideas for stories that you told or acted out with toys. A story you were telling might have gone on and on until you got tired of it.

As you get older, your stories start to have more **focus.** You have a purpose in mind and certain ideas that you want to express. You want an audience to enjoy your stories, too. The **purpose** of a story is usually to entertain readers. Other kinds of writing have other purposes, such as to inform or to persuade.

Read the beginning of this student's story. What problem or conflict do you think the story will focus on? How might the writer have gotten the idea for the story?

Student Model

Roger was younger than the others in his class, but he seemed far older than his years. Not only did he know more than the other kids, but he was responsible and sensible, too. It was enough to drive his friends crazy.

"You're making us look bad," Celia told Roger one day. "You ace every test, you clean up your room, and you never forget Mother's Day. How can the rest of us compete?"

Roger looked at Celia. She and Moose and Freddy were his best friends in the world. They did everything together. Celia couldn't really be mad at him, could she?

> Who is the main character?

> The dialogue includes details that relate to the story's focus.

> What problem does the main character face?

How to Focus Your Writing

Focus/Ideas Strategies	How to Use the Strategies
Narrow your topic.	• Brainstorm ideas for writing. Then choose a main idea or a central conflict. State it near the beginning of your composition.
Keep your purpose and audience in mind.	• Stick to your purpose of entertaining, informing, or persuading. Use words and ideas that will be interesting to your audience.
Stay on the topic.	• Make sure each detail relates directly to the topic. At the end of your composition, restate the main idea, or show how the conflict is resolved.

Try This! Brainstorm problems or conflicts that could be the focus of a story—for example, getting lost in a mall or having an argument with a friend. Choose one problem, and state it in a complete sentence, giving the names of the characters involved.

Writing Forms

A story is a fictional narrative usually told in time order and centering around a problem and its solution. It contains a beginning, middle, and ending.

For more about stories, see pages 56–57.

Focus/Ideas

To practice your craft, write a short story that focuses on a problem and its resolution.

Writing Prompt

Write a short story about a character who must solve a problem and complete a task. Use descriptive details and dialogue that support your purpose and focus.

> **Strategies**
> **Good Writers Use**
>
> • Focus on your purpose for writing: to entertain.
> • Think about your own experiences for ideas.
> • Use dialogue and description to make your characters seem lifelike.

Prewrite

Use a story map to plan your story.

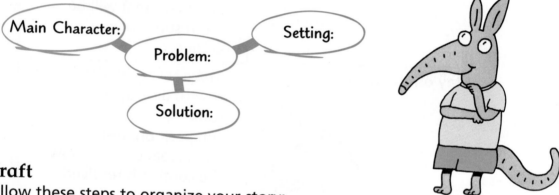

Main Character:

Problem:

Setting:

Solution:

Draft

Follow these steps to organize your story:

STEP 1 **Introduce the setting and characters.** Give details about the time, place, and characters.

STEP 2 **Provide the problem.** Show the main character's problem.

STEP 3 **Solve the problem.** Show the steps the character takes to solve the problem. Include vivid details and dialogue.

STEP 4 **Conclude your story.** Once the problem is solved, show how the characters feel.

Revise

Read over the draft of your short story. Use this checklist to help you revise your writing:

- ☑ Do all the details relate to your focus?
- ☑ Do you need to add details to make the events more interesting?
- ☑ Does the sequence of events make sense?
- ☑ In dialogue, is it always clear who is speaking?

Proofread

Use this checklist as you proofread your story:

- ☑ Have you capitalized proper nouns?
- ☑ Have you used quotation marks correctly in dialogue?
- ☑ Have you started a new paragraph when the speaker changes?
- ☑ Have you indented the first line of each paragraph?
- ☑ Have you checked your spelling?

✌	delete text
∧	insert text
↺	move text
¶	new paragraph
≡	capitalize
/	lowercase
◯	correct spelling

Publish and Reflect

Make a final copy of your story, and prepare to read it aloud to a group. Ask your classmates to tell what they like best about the story. Discuss whether you stayed focused on the main problem or conflict. In your Writer's Journal, write what you learned.

Organization

Just as organizing your work space helps you work, organizing your ideas helps you write. You can organize writing in many ways. You usually organize events in **time order**, from beginning to end. You might organize a description of a place in **space order**, for example, from left to right or top to bottom. You might organize persuasive writing by **reasons**, from most to least important, or from least to most important. You may also group ideas in **categories**, such as likes and dislikes. With any pattern of organization, you can use **transition words,** such as *first, next,* and *in addition,* to help your reader follow your ideas.

As you read this student's how-to essay, think about how the information is organized.

Student Model

If you are looking for an interesting hobby, you might find it right in your mailbox. Stamp collecting is popular all over the world. It is easy to start your own collection.

First, decide what kinds of stamps to collect. Next, you will need to buy a stamp album. You might also invest in a magnifying glass and some tweezers. Finally, begin collecting. You can tell friends and family to save interesting stamps for you, check the post office for new stamps, and look on the Internet for stamp offers.

Now you're ready to begin your new hobby. As your collection grows, you'll learn a lot!

The writer begins by introducing the topic in an interesting way.

The writer uses time order for the steps.

What transition words does the writer use?

How to Organize Ideas

Strategies	Applying the Strategies
Order ideas clearly.	Put ideas in an order that makes sense, such as time order, space order, categories, or order of importance.
Use transition words.	**Time-Order Words:** after, before, finally, first, last, later, next, now, soon, then **Space-Order Words:** above, around, below, here, inside, next to, over, there, under **Words That Show Categories:** in the same way, similarly, on the other hand, in contrast, another **Words That Show Order of Importance:** first, last, primarily, second, third

Try This! A news article often uses both order of importance and time order. It may begin with the most important part of the news story and then tell other parts of the story in time order. Find two news articles in a newspaper. Tell how each is organized.

Writing Forms

A how-to essay lists all the materials needed for a project and uses numbers or transition words to put ideas in step-by-step order.

For more about how-to writing, see pages 70–71.

Organization

Practice your craft by writing a how-to essay that puts ideas in order and is easy to follow.

Writing Prompt

Write a how-to essay telling your classmates how to start a new hobby or activity. State your topic in the introduction, and list all the steps. Include details and examples to explain the steps.

Strategies Good Writers Use

- Decide on your purpose and audience.
- Imagine yourself doing the task you are explaining.
- If something must be done a certain way, tell the reader why.

Prewrite

Use a graphic to organize your information.

Purpose:
Tell why you are writing.
Audience:
Tell who might read your writing.

Topic:
Explain your topic in a sentence or two.

Steps:
Write steps in order.
1.
2.
3.

Draft

Follow these steps to help you write your essay:

STEP 1 **Introduce your topic** in an interesting way. Tell why your audience might want to try the activity.

STEP 2 **List all materials and equipment.** Explain items that might be unfamiliar to your audience.

STEP 3 **Describe each main step.** Write each step as a topic sentence for a separate paragraph. Add details and examples.

STEP 4 **Write a concluding paragraph.** Restate your topic. Encourage your audience to try the activity.

Revise

Read over the draft of your how-to essay. Can you improve the essay to make it easier to understand? Use this checklist to help you revise and proofread your instructions:

☑ Does your essay begin in a way that grabs the reader's attention?

☑ Are the steps in an order that makes sense?

☑ Should you add or leave out some details to make the instructions easier to follow?

☑ Did you use transition words to help your reader complete the steps?

Proofread

Use this checklist as you proofread your essay:

☑ Have you used capitalization and punctuation correctly?

☑ Have you used singular and plural nouns correctly?

☑ Have you used apostrophes in possessive nouns but not in plural nouns?

☑ Have you used a dictionary to check your spelling?

↧	delete text
⋀	insert text
↺	move text
¶	new paragraph
≡	capitalize
/	lowercase
◯	correct spelling

Publish and Reflect

After making a final copy of your how-to essay, share it with a partner by reading it aloud. Ask your partner whether he or she would be able to follow your directions. Discuss what you like about your partner's essay, and talk about strategies for writing clearer directions in the future. Record your ideas in your Writer's Journal.

Voice

You have your own way of expressing yourself. It comes through in the way that you speak, dress, and act, and it shows in your writing as well. The way you express yourself in writing is called your **voice.**

Your personal voice makes your writing different from anyone else's. It reveals your opinions, feelings, impressions, and beliefs. You can share your personality with your reader just by the way you use words.

Read this descriptive paragraph. Think about how the writer shows that she cares about her subject.

Student Model

On my street there is a beautiful little garden where my neighbors grow vegetables. Mrs. Santiago has a tomato patch with tomatoes as round and red as the setting sun. Sometimes she slices a tomato right there in the garden and gives me a piece to eat, all juicy and warm in my mouth. Old Mr. Williams grows five different kinds of lettuce. I love to look at all the different shades of green, from pale and delicate to dark and hearty. Mrs. Finn lets me help her pull earthy-smelling orange carrots from the moist soil. Our neighborhood garden is a feast for the eyes and the nose, as well as for the appetite.

> The writer establishes her viewpoint.

> The writer chooses words that appeal to the senses.

> The writer expresses her feelings and opinions.

Try This! Pretend that you walk blindfolded into the garden described above. What do you smell? Now take your blindfold off. What do you see?

How to Develop Your Personal Voice

Strategies	Examples
Use figurative language and imagery. Common types of figurative language are **similes, metaphors,** and **personification**. **Imagery** is vivid language that helps the reader form a mental picture.	**Simile:** The baby's skin was as smooth as a flower petal. **Metaphor:** The clouds were puffs of smoke. **Personification:** The trees danced in the wind. **Imagery:** A frigid wind rattled the bare branches.
Include sensory details. **Sensory details** appeal to the five senses: sight, hearing, touch, smell, and taste. They help the reader share your experience.	**Sight and touch:** The orange rock lay heavy in my hand. **Smell:** Barney smelled the unmistakable, eye-watering stench of a skunk.
Express your own viewpoint. Choose words that suggest emotions, such as happiness, fear, or fascination.	**Fear:** The terrifying beast stalked its victim.

Reading ↔ Writing Connection

Look for vivid sensory details in stories, advertisements, and poems. Choose several words that fit each sensory category. Add them to your Word Bank.

Voice

To practice your craft, write a descriptive paragraph using personal voice.

Writing Prompt

Write a descriptive paragraph about something from nature for your classmates. Include figurative language, imagery, and sensory details to help your reader create a mental image. Choose words carefully to express your viewpoint.

Strategies
Good Writers Use

- Remember your purpose and audience.
- Include details that make your viewpoint clear.

Prewrite

Organize your ideas in a web.

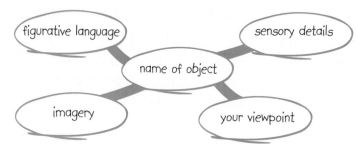

figurative language

sensory details

name of object

imagery

your viewpoint

Draft

Follow these steps:

STEP 1 **Begin with a topic sentence.** Identify the object, and place it in a setting.

STEP 2 **Write in your own voice.** Use language that helps your reader understand your view of the object.

STEP 3 **Sum up the experience.** Conclude with an expression of your viewpoint.

Revise

Read over the draft of your descriptive paragraph. Can you add anything to create a more vivid picture for your reader? Use this checklist to help you revise your paragraph:

☑ Will your readers be able to picture the object or scene in their minds?

☑ Can you add figurative language or imagery to your description?

☑ Does your viewpoint come through clearly?

ℓ	delete text
⌃	insert text
↺	move text
¶	new paragraph
≡	capitalize
/	lowercase
◯	correct spelling

Proofread

Use this checklist as you proofread your paragraph:

☑ Have you used correct capitalization and punctuation?

☑ Have you checked to see that every sentence has a subject and a predicate?

☑ Have you used compound subjects to combine sentences where possible?

☑ Have you used a dictionary to check your spelling?

Publish and Reflect

Make a final copy of your paragraph, and share it with several classmates. Tell what you like best about your classmates' descriptions. Point out examples of figurative language, imagery, and sensory details. Discuss each other's viewpoints and how they are expressed. In your journal, write some ideas about improving your own descriptive writing and developing your personal voice.

Word Choice

Good writers try to use **exact words,** or the right words for what they want to say. Suppose you want to tell how you felt after riding in a bicycle race: Were you *tired,* or were you *exhausted?* You would choose the word that has the exact meaning you want.

Good writers also use **vivid words.** These are words that create strong, clear images in the reader's mind. For example, if you are describing someone who is small, you might talk about *stubby fingers, delicate feet,* or *tiny features.* If the person talks loudly, you might refer to his or her *rough growl, boisterous laugh,* or *jangling chatter.*

Read this student's character sketch. What does the writer's word choice tell you about the character?

Student Model

Marcus's mother, Mrs. Blake, was not a tall woman, but she stood straight as a soldier. When she walked, her small feet tapped rapidly and lightly. Her voice rang out in firm, clear tones, leaving no doubt that she expected Marcus to listen.

Marcus often noticed his mother's large, dark eyes. They flashed like lightning when she was angry. More often, though, they crinkled with laughter. Sometimes she laughed so hard that tears streamed down her face.

Mrs. Blake loved to cook. She made crumbly corn muffins, flaky hot biscuits, and stew so delicious it made Marcus hungry just to smell it.

Notice the use of vivid verbs and adjectives to describe Mrs. Blake's actions and speech.

What does the phrase "flashed like lightning" tell you about Mrs. Blake's temper?

How does the writer feel about Mrs. Blake? How can you tell?

Strategies for Choosing Words

Strategies	Examples
Use exact words.	Use words like **bounces** or **trudges** to tell how a person walks. Use specific nouns like **cottage** or **skyscraper** instead of a general noun like **building.**
Use vivid descriptive words and phrases.	Use words like **brawny** or **frail, cautiously** or **heedlessly,** and phrases like **hair as soft as flower petals.**
Express a tone, or attitude.	The overall tone may be humorous, playful, sad, angry, respectful, sympathetic, and so on.

Try This! Choose a place in your school, such as the library, the cafeteria, the playground, or the principal's office. Imagine yourself there, and write several sentences about what you see, hear, touch, and, perhaps, smell or taste. Rather than tell how you feel about the place, show it through vivid and exact words.

Reading ↔ Writing Connection

Poets choose their words very carefully. Find a book of poetry, and read several poems. Choose interesting or vivid words to add to your Word Bank.

Word Choice

Now it's your turn! Follow the steps on these two pages to write a fantasy that uses exact and vivid words.

 **Writing Prompt**

Suppose you become something else for a day—for example, a dog, an ant, a car, a backpack, a pencil. Write about your day.

Strategies Good Writers Use

- Think of details that will interest and surprise your readers.
- Let your own voice and tone come through.

Prewrite
Brainstorm details for your fantasy, and organize them in a web.

Draft
Follow these steps to organize your writing.

What I noticed first

My Day as a _____

What I saw, heard, felt, and smelled

What I did

STEP 1 Introduce the topic.
Describe what you noticed first and how you felt.

STEP 2 Tell about events.
Tell the main things that happened to you during the day. Use details that appeal to the senses.

STEP 3 Draw some conclusions.
Tell what you learned from the experience or how you felt when it was over.

Writing Tip

Use your Word Bank to find vivid words to help readers picture the scenes and events you describe.

Revise

Read over the draft of your fantasy. Do you want to add, delete, or change anything? Use this checklist to help you revise your work:

- ☑ Will your reader get a clear picture of the experience?
- ☑ Should you replace vague words with more exact ones?
- ☑ Can you add any details that appeal to the senses?
- ☑ Did you stick to the first-person point of view?

Proofread

Use the checklist as you proofread your writing:

- ☑ Have you used verb forms correctly?
- ☑ Have you capitalized proper nouns?
- ☑ Have you punctuated sentences correctly?
- ☑ Have you used a dictionary to check your spelling?

✐	delete text
∧	insert text
↻	move text
¶	new paragraph
≡	capitalize
/	lowercase
◯	correct spelling

Publish and Reflect

Make a final copy of your fantasy, and read it aloud to a partner or a group of classmates. Point out vivid words and phrases in your classmates' writing. In your Writer's Journal, tell what you liked most about writing a fantasy.

Development

Adding reasons and details to explain your ideas is called **development**. Everything you write will be improved by adding details. It is most important to develop your ideas clearly and logically when you write to persuade. When you want to persuade someone to do something or to agree with your point of view, you must do more than express your opinion. You must support your opinion with reasons and facts.

Read this student's persuasive letter. Think about how the writer develops her ideas and supports her opinion.

Student Model

To the Editor:

    I have been reading about the plan to build a new parking lot on Ledge Street. I believe that this is a big mistake.

    To build the parking lot, we would have to cut down many trees. These trees help protect us from air and noise pollution.

    In addition, there is already too much traffic in that area. I walk there every day and often see traffic jams and minor accidents.

    I hope the readers of this newspaper will ask their representatives on the City Council to vote against this plan.

              Sincerely,

              Melissa Martino

What is Melissa's opinion?

What two reasons does Melissa give to support her opinion?

What details does Melissa give to develop her reasons?

How to Develop Ideas

Strategies	Questions to Ask Yourself
Identify your purpose and audience.	What opinion do I want to express? Whom do I want to persuade?
Use reasons and details.	What reasons can I give to show why others should agree with my opinion? What details can I give to support each of my reasons?
Stay on the topic.	Do all of my reasons and details clearly support my opinion?

Try This! Choose a magazine or newspaper ad that includes a drawing or photograph. Write a paragraph analyzing the persuasive effect of these parts of the ad: the setting, the facial expressions of the people, and the size and color of the words used.

Writing Forms

Persuasive writing offers strong reasons to support an opinion and develops those reasons with details, facts, and examples.

For more about persuasive writing, see pages 82–83.

Development

To practice your craft, write a persuasive essay that supports an opinion.

Writing Prompt

Write a persuasive essay urging your classmates to do (or keep doing) something that you think is good for them. State your opinion, and support your idea with specific reasons and examples. Conclude by asking your classmates to take action.

Strategies Good Writers Use

- Decide on your purpose.
- Brainstorm reasons that will persuade your audience.
- Ask yourself what objections your audience might have to your opinion and answer them.

Prewrite

Use a graphic to plan your essay.

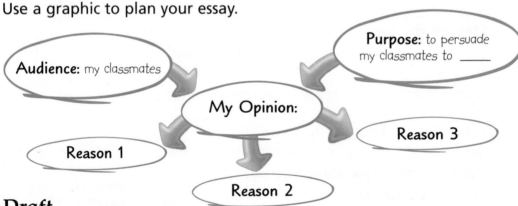

Draft

Follow these steps to draft your essay:

STEP 1 **Introduce your topic** in a way that makes your audience want to read on.

STEP 2 **State your opinion** clearly and directly.

STEP 3 **Support your opinion.** Organize reasons in order of importance from least to greatest. Include facts and examples.

STEP 4 **Conclude with a call to action.** Restate your opinion. Tell your audience what to do.

Revise

Read over your persuasive essay. Can you revise your essay to make it clearer? Use this checklist to help you revise your work:

- ☑ Could your reader easily restate your opinion?
- ☑ Are your reasons organized into paragraphs?
- ☑ Have you included enough details, examples, or facts to support each reason? (If not, add more details.)
- ☑ Have you stayed on the topic?

Proofread

Use this checklist as you proofread your essay:

- ☑ Do your subjects and verbs agree?
- ☑ Have you capitalized and punctuated sentences correctly?
- ☑ Have you spelled irregular verbs correctly?
- ☑ Have you used a dictionary to check your spelling?

℮	delete text
∧	insert text
⟳	move text
¶	new paragraph
≡	capitalize
/	lowercase
◯	correct spelling

Publish and Reflect

Make a final copy of your persuasive essay, and share it with a partner. Tell what you like best about your partner's essay. Try to identify your partner's opinion, reasons, and details that strengthen those reasons. Discuss why development is important in writing. Record your ideas in your Writer's Journal.

Effective Sentences

When you talk about yourself, do you begin every sentence with *I*? Your listeners would doze off if you did. As you speak, you naturally vary your sentences to add interest and emphasis and to make your meaning clear.

Effective sentences are important in writing, too. When you write, your sentences should be varied and interesting. They should not only capture and hold a reader's attention, but they should also be clear enough to communicate your meaning.

As you read the beginning of this student's personal narrative, think about how the writer uses a variety of sentences to capture the reader's interest and to make her meaning clear.

> The writer begins with a sentence that invites you to read on.

Student Model

My love of kites began one day last March. It was a beautiful, breezy day, and everyone in the neighborhood was outside. I was sketching a robin in my backyard when a loud noise startled me. An eagle was swooping down from the sky. As it fell, it screamed "Waaaah!" I leaped to my feet and ran. It lay still. When I looked more closely, I realized that the eagle was made of painted paper!

> Some sentences are long, and others are short. One sentence uses a quotation to add interest.

> Where does the writer use a compound predicate?

Try This! Choose a piece of your own writing. Find your shortest sentence and your longest sentence. If you used short, choppy sentences, see where you can combine sentences for better flow.

How to Write Effective Sentences

Strategies	Applying the Strategies	Examples
Write an interesting opening sentence.	Write a sentence that tells what you are writing about and sparks your reader's interest.	"What's going on?" I wondered when I saw the big crowd.
Use different sentence types.	Use statements, questions, and exclamations.	The ostrich is amazing! Did you know that an adult ostrich is faster than a racehorse?
Use different sentence structures.	Include compound subjects and predicates, as well as compound and complex sentences.	I swung the bat with all my strength, but I missed the ball.

Try This! Find a piece written in the first person. Analyze the first two paragraphs. How does the author vary his or her sentences? Are the sentences effective? Explain your thinking.

Writing Forms

A personal narrative uses the first-person point of view to tell a story about the author's own experience.

For more about personal narratives, see page 68.

Effective Sentences

To practice your craft, write a personal narrative that uses effective sentences.

(Writing Prompt)

Write a personal narrative telling your classmates about a time when you were surprised by something. It might be a good or a bad surprise. Give your narrative a beginning, a middle, and an ending.

Strategies Good Writers Use

- Write about something that interests you.
- Write in the first person, and use a strong, natural voice.
- Use dialogue to add sentence variety.

Prewrite

Use a flowchart to help you plan your writing.

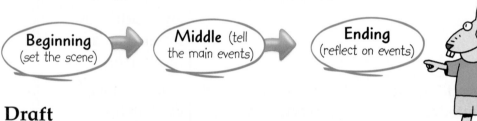

Beginning (set the scene) **Middle** (tell the main events) **Ending** (reflect on events)

Draft

Use these steps to organize your narrative:

STEP 1 **Introduce your topic** in a way that grabs your audience's attention. Write the beginning of your narrative.

STEP 2 **Write the middle of your narrative.** Put events in the order in which they happened. Remember to vary your sentences.

STEP 3 **Write the ending.** Explain what the events in your narrative meant to you.

Revise

Read over the draft of your personal narrative. Do you see ways to make your sentences more effective? Use this checklist to help you revise your writing:

☑ Is your opening sentence strong and direct?

☑ Have you used a variety of sentence types?

☑ Will your sentences capture and hold your reader's interest?

☑ Could you combine some sentences to vary sentence length?

Proofread

Use this checklist as you proofread your narrative:

☑ Have you used capitalization and punctuation correctly?

☑ Have you used correct verb tenses?

☑ Have you used commas correctly in compound and complex sentences?

☑ Have you used a dictionary to check your spelling?

ℰ	delete text
∧	insert text
◯	move text
¶	new paragraph
☰	capitalize
/	lowercase
◯	correct spelling

Publish and Reflect

Make a final copy of your personal narrative. Illustrate your narrative with drawings or photographs. Over the next few days, try to read several of your classmates' narratives. Notice whether their sentences are clear and effective. Think about how you might use their ideas to improve your own writing. Record your thoughts in your Writer's Journal.

Effective Paragraphs

Reading a story or a report that is all one paragraph would not be much fun. The use of **paragraphs** to group ideas helps make writing easy to understand and follow.

In expository writing, most paragraphs have a topic sentence that states the main idea. This is the broadest, or most general, idea in the paragraph. The other sentences give details about the topic sentence.

Read this paragraph from a student's research report. Notice how the sentences work together to explain the main idea.

Student Model

Prospecting for gold was hard work. People thought they could simply pick up gold from the ground. Instead, they had to sift through handfuls of dirt, sand, and gravel, washing it with water in pans or special wooden boxes. Because the flakes of gold were heavy, they sank to the bottom. Prospectors might take hours or even days to sift through a small patch of ground. It took a long, long time to find just a little bit of gold.

A topic sentence tells the main idea.

Notice the transition word *instead*.

What details are used to support the main idea?

The writer concludes with a summary sentence.

Try This! Look at a magazine article. Try to determine why the writer broke it into paragraphs the way he or she did. Locate each topic sentence. Do the remaining sentences in the paragraph support that topic sentence?

How to Write Effective Paragraphs

Strategies	Examples
Write a topic sentence, and write additional sentences to give details that relate to it.	**Topic sentence**: Because of the gold rush, California's population grew rapidly. **Details:** There were 15,000 settlers in early 1848. There were more than 100,000 at the end of 1849.
Give information in the correct order, or sequence.	When gold was discovered in California in 1848, the news spread around the world. By 1849, thousands of people had rushed to California, dreaming of becoming rich.
Use words and phrases that show how ideas connect to each other.	Most people traveled to California by covered wagon, **while** others made the long journey by ship.

Reading ↔ Writing Connection

An introduction and a conclusion are special kinds of paragraphs. Find a magazine article or a speech that you think has an effective introduction and conclusion. In your Writer's Journal, note the methods that the writer used in these paragraphs.

Effective Paragraphs

To practice your craft, write an informational report that uses effective paragraphs.

Writing Prompt

Choose a specific event in American history that you think everyone should know about. Use resources to write a report that tells what happened. Think about what you might do to make the information interesting to readers your age.

Strategies Good Writers Use

- Narrow the topic to an idea that can be covered in a short report.
- Remember your purpose and audience.
- Try to write about your topic in a new way. Include your own viewpoint.

Prewrite

Make a chart to plan your report.

Main Topic:	
Subtopic	Facts and Details
Subtopic	Facts and Details

Draft

Follow these steps:

STEP 1 **Introduce the topic** in the first paragraph.

STEP 2 **Organize the subtopics.** Write a paragraph for each subtopic. Give each paragraph a topic sentence.

STEP 3 **Add facts and details** that support each subtopic.

STEP 4 **Write a conclusion** that tells why you think the event is interesting or important.

Revise

Read over the draft of your informational report. Use this checklist to help you revise your paragraphs:

- ☑ Does each body paragraph contain a topic sentence?
- ☑ Do the details in each paragraph tell about its topic sentence?
- ☑ Are your paragraphs in an order that makes sense?
- ☑ Are your introduction and conclusion effective?

ℓ	delete text
∧	insert text
↰	move text
¶	new paragraph
≡	capitalize
/	lowercase
◯	correct spelling

Proofread

Use this checklist as you proofread your report:

- ☑ Have you used capitalization and punctuation correctly?
- ☑ Do your subjects and verbs agree in number?
- ☑ Have you indented the first line of each paragraph?
- ☑ Have you used a dictionary to check your spelling?

Publish and Reflect

Make a final copy of your informational report. Then deliver the report orally to the class. Answer any questions your classmates have. What do their questions show about their understanding of your report? Write your reflections in your Writer's Journal.

Conventions

Written language follows certain conventions that help make it clear for readers. A **convention** is a kind of rule, or an accepted way of doing something. For example, we write in sentences from left to right on the page. Your writing would be very hard to read if it did not follow these conventions.

When you proofread, you check to see how well you used the conventions of written English.

Proofreading Strategies

Wait before proofreading. Avoid proofreading your composition immediately after you have written it. Come back to it later, and read it as if someone else had written it.

Proofread in stages. You might want to follow these steps:

1. Read your composition and think about its meaning. Make sure your **sentences** are complete and make sense. Make sure you have indented **paragraphs.**

2. Next, focus on **grammar, usage, capitalization,** and **punctuation.** How would you change this sentence? *The flote and the daft, was clooning in the worstest garn ever.* You can correct the grammar and punctuation in this sentence without knowing what it means.

3. Last, focus on **spelling.** Try reading backwards to check your spelling. Circle any words you are not sure of, and look them up in a dictionary.

Proofread with a partner. A classmate may see problems that you have overlooked.

Proofreading Checklist

Sentences and Paragraphs

☑ Does every sentence have a subject and a predicate?

☑ Have I avoided run-on sentences?

☑ Have I used the correct form for compound and complex sentences?

☑ Does each sentence begin with a capital letter and end with the correct end mark?

☑ Have I indented each paragraph?

Grammar, Usage, Capitalization, and Punctuation

☑ Do my verbs agree with their subjects?

☑ Have I used the correct forms of irregular verbs?

☑ Do my pronouns agree with their antecedents?

☑ Have I used the correct form of adjectives and adverbs that compare?

☑ Have I capitalized proper nouns and the pronoun *I*?

☑ Have I used commas to join the parts of compound and complex sentences?

☑ Have I used apostrophes correctly in possessive nouns and contractions?

Spelling

☑ Am I sure of the spelling of every word?

☑ Have I always used the correct homophone?

☑ Have I spelled noun plurals correctly?

Presenting Your Work

Some writing is private. When you write in your diary or make notes for yourself, that writing is not meant for anyone but you. However, most writing is meant to be **published**, or made public.

There are many ways to publish your writing. Some methods depend on the type of writing it is. Other methods are appropriate for any type of writing. Here are some ideas:

Strategies Good Writers Use

- Think about your audience. Should you publish in cursive or manuscript printing? Should you use large or small type?
- Consider whether illustrations or diagrams might make your ideas easier to understand.

Publishing Ideas for Any Type of Writing

- Read it aloud.
- Have a friend read it silently.
- Post it on a bulletin board.
- Attach it to an e-mail.

Publishing Ideas for Descriptive Writing

- Use art materials to make an illustrated brochure.
- Take or find photographs to illustrate the work.
- Make your writing the centerpiece of a collage or quilt.
- Find music to enhance your writing. Record yourself reading to music.
- Choreograph a dance to accompany your oral reading.

Publishing Ideas for Narrative Writing

- Produce your story as a play.

- Make a videotape of your story as a play or a Readers Theatre.

- Make an illustrated, covered book for the classroom library.

- Read your work aloud to children in a kindergarten class.

- Submit your writing to your school literary magazine.

- Enter your story in a writing contest.

- Read aloud and have friends pantomime the action.

- Include your story in a classroom anthology.

Technology

If you use a word processor to publish your writing, use **Format** to choose a font that is readable and appropriate for your audience. Usually, you will want to double-space your material. For longer documents, you may **Insert** page numbers automatically.

Publishing Ideas for Informational Writing

• Prepare a PowerPoint™ presentation based on your report.

• Create a table display for the classroom or for a school fair.

• Work with classmates to make a book on a broad topic.

• Make a poster for the school hallway.

• Take over as "teacher" and instruct your classmates.

• Use your report as the voiceover for a videotape.

Publishing Ideas for Persuasive Writing

• Send your work as a letter to the editor of your school or local paper.

• Give a speech to your class or at a school assembly.

• Present your ideas orally to a club or to the student council.

• Hold a classroom debate on the topic.

• Publish your work on your school's web site.

*S*trategies *G*ood *W*riters *U*se

• Leave adequate margins.
• Write legibly.
• Indent paragraphs.
• Put your name on your work.

Strategies for Making an Oral Presentation	Applying the Strategies
Make note cards.	• Write each main idea on a note card. Include any major details. Write clearly and in large print.
Use visual aids.	• Consider adding pictures, charts, diagrams, music, video, or PowerPoint™ slides.
Practice.	• Use a mirror, or present your talk to a friend. Look for places you might stress words or vary your rate or volume.
Present confidently.	• Remember that you are the expert on your own topic. Make eye contact with your audience. Use your note cards only as reference points. Speak loudly and clearly. Be prepared to answer questions.

Strategies for Listeners Identify the speaker's main idea, purpose, and point of view. Notice whether the speaker's opinion has enough support. Decide whether you agree with the speaker or admire the presentation.

Uppercase and Lowercase
Manuscript Alphabet

Uppercase and Lowercase
Cursive Alphabet

A B C D E F G H I
J K L M N O P Q R
S T U V W X Y Z

A B C D E F G H I
J K L M N O P Q R
S T U V W X Y Z

a b c d e f g h i
j k l m n o p q r
s t u v w x y z

a b c d e f g h i
j k l m n o p q r
s t u v w x y z

D'Nealian
Cursive Alphabet

A B C D E F G H
I J K L M N O P
2 R S T U V W
X Y Z

a b c d e f g h
i j k l m n o p
q r s t u v w
x y z

Elements of Handwriting

Shape
Letters must be shaped correctly to make your writing readable. Write each letter using the correct shape.

correct

radio

incorrect

radio

Spacing of Letters
The letters in a word should not be too close together or too far apart. Space between words and sentences must be even. Remember to leave room for one spacer ☐ between words and sentences.

correct

Who is it?

incorrect

Who is it?

Position
As you write, make the bottom parts of the uppercase and lowercase letters sit evenly on the bottom line.

correct

St. Louis

incorrect

St. Louis

Elements of Handwriting

Size and Proportion

Each letter should be the correct size. Letters and letter parts should be the same in relation to other letters. Most tall letters touch both top line and bottom line. Most short letters touch the imaginary midline and the bottom line.

correct

grip

incorrect

grip

When it becomes necessary to write smaller than you usually do, reduce the size of the letters, but keep the proportion the same.

Slant

To make your writing neat and legible, slant all your letters in the same direction. Keep your paper in the proper position, and hold your pen correctly.

correct

fiddle

incorrect

fiddle

Stroke

All your strokes should be smooth and flowing. Letters and joining strokes should be smooth and even.

correct

bit

unsteady

bit

too light

bit

too dark

bit

Using E-Mail

Sending electronic mail, or e-mail, is a convenient way to communicate. However, there are a few important things you should remember about using e-mail.

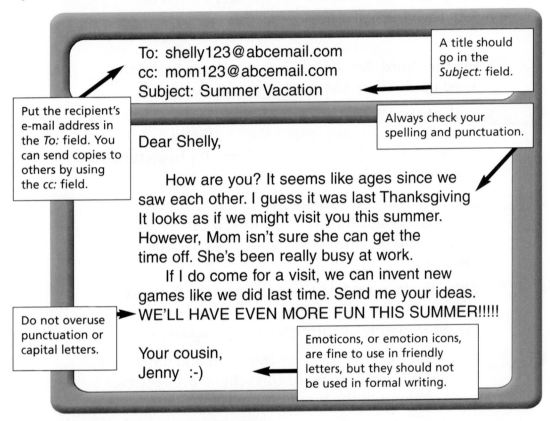

To: shelly123@abcemail.com
cc: mom123@abcemail.com
Subject: Summer Vacation

A title should go in the *Subject:* field.

Put the recipient's e-mail address in the *To:* field. You can send copies to others by using the *cc:* field.

Always check your spelling and punctuation.

Dear Shelly,

    How are you? It seems like ages since we saw each other. I guess it was last Thanksgiving It looks as if we might visit you this summer. However, Mom isn't sure she can get the time off. She's been really busy at work.
    If I do come for a visit, we can invent new games like we did last time. Send me your ideas. WE'LL HAVE EVEN MORE FUN THIS SUMMER!!!!!

Do not overuse punctuation or capital letters.

Your cousin,
Jenny :-)

Emoticons, or emotion icons, are fine to use in friendly letters, but they should not be used in formal writing.

E-Mail Manners and Safety

- Remember that you are writing a letter. Think about and use what you know about writing letters.

- Don't type in all capital letters. It looks as if you are shouting.

- Immediately tell an adult if you get a message that makes you uncomfortable.

- Never give your e-mail address or other personal information to strangers.

Spelling Strategies

Some people seem to be naturally good at spelling. Others struggle to spell simple words. The more you read and write, the better your spelling will become. The steps listed below can help you learn to spell a new word:

STEP 1 **Say the Word.** Remember how you have heard the word used. Think about what it means.

STEP 2 **Look at the Word.** Look for prefixes, suffixes, or other word parts you know. Think about other words that are related in meaning and spelling. Try to picture the word in your mind.

STEP 3 **Spell the Word to Yourself.** Think about the way each sound is spelled. For example, long *a* can be spelled *a, ai, a-e, ay, eigh,* and so on. Notice any unusual spelling.

STEP 4 **Write the Word While Looking at It.** Check the way you have formed the letters. If you have not written the word clearly or correctly, write it again.

STEP 5 **Check Your Learning.** Cover the word and write it. If you did not spell the word correctly, practice these steps again until the word becomes familiar to you.

Try This! Choose five of the commonly misspelled words below. Use the five steps above to practice spelling the words you chose.

assignment	fault	opposite
congratulated	language	tomorrow
different	library	weird

Strategies for Making a Personal Spelling List	Applying the Strategies
Check your writing for words you have misspelled.	• Circle each misspelled word.
Find out how to spell the word correctly.	• Use a dictionary, glossary, or thesaurus to look up the word. • Ask a teacher or classmate how to spell the word.
Write the word in your journal.	• Spell the word correctly. • Write a definition, synonym, or antonym to help you recall the meaning of the word. • Use the word in a sentence.
Use your spelling list to check your spelling as you write.	• Try to use new words often in your writing.

Technology

If you use a computer spell checker, remember that it cannot distinguish between homophones. For example, the spell checker does not know whether you mean *their*, *there*, or *they're*—as long as you spell the word correctly, it will not catch a mistake.

Peer Conferencing

In a **peer conference**, students come together to listen, respond, and share their writing. Peer conferences are most useful during the revising part of the writing process. You may take what your classmates say and apply it to improve your written work.

Strategies for Sharing Your Work	Applying the Strategies
• **Make copies of your work.**	• Give each person in the peer conference a copy.
• **Read the work aloud.**	• You may prefer to have someone else read it, or you might have everyone read it silently. If you read your own work, don't add comments that aren't part of the writing.
• **Respond to the work of others.**	• Be specific. Tell what you like and why. Tell what doesn't work and why. • Be polite. Don't criticize without giving ideas for improvement.

Strategies for Reading Aloud

• Speak clearly and loudly.
• Match your voice to the events or feelings you are expressing.
• Make eye contact with your audience.
• Use gestures and facial expressions.

Strategies for Listening During a Peer Conference	Applying the Strategies
• **Listen actively.**	• Pay attention as the work is being read. Think about the main idea, the supporting details, and the language used. • Try to summarize the writing in your mind before you respond to it.
• **Take notes.**	• Jot quick notes when you're listening to the work of others. • As classmates make suggestions about your writing, write them down.
• **Keep an open mind.**	• Do not reject what your classmates tell you about your work. Try to understand their reasons. If necessary, ask them to explain themselves. • When you listen to someone else's work, don't think about how you would have written it. Remember that personal voice varies from person to person.

Using Rubrics

Have you ever wondered how your teacher grades writing assignments? Your teacher probably uses a kind of checklist or chart called a **rubric**.

Rubrics list traits to look for in writing. A paper that has all the traits earns the highest score. The highest score may be 4, 5, or 6.

You can use rubrics during writing to help you earn your highest score.

Before Writing
- Review the rubric to remind yourself of the traits of good writing.
- Keep these traits in mind as you prepare to write.

During Writing
- Check to see how well your draft matches the list of key traits.
- Put marks next to any trait that is missing from your draft.
- Use your marked rubric as you revise your draft.

After Writing
- Check your finished work against the rubric.
- If your work still can be improved, revise your writing again.

Strategies Good Writers Use

- Poor handwriting can make even good writing difficult to understand. Don't lose points because your writing can't be read.
- Remember that spelling counts! When in doubt, use a dictionary to check your spelling.

Sometimes a rubric shows just the highest score. Here is a sample rubric for a research report. The highest score is 6 points.

SCORE OF 6 ★★★★★★

- ★ The research report fits the purpose for writing. The audience it was written for would understand it.
- ★ The report has a clear beginning that introduces the topic. The middle sections give logically organized information and ideas about the topic. The ending summarizes or draws a conclusion.
- ★ The report presents ideas and information from a variety of sources. The writer uses his or her own words.
- ★ The report has description, rich details, or narrative parts that add information about the topic. The ideas are interesting.
- ★ The report has transition words and phrases that help the reader understand how the ideas are related.
- ★ The sentences are written in a variety of ways to make the writing interesting to read.
- ★ The report has few errors in spelling, grammar, and punctuation.

What other traits do you think are important in a research report?

Writing for Tests

Demand writing is writing that is based on a **prompt**, or a given topic. Demand writing is usually timed. Standardized tests often include this kind of timed writing.

The prompt tells you the topic of your writing assignment. It also tells you the purpose and form of your writing.

Model Writing Prompt

It's hard to be the "new kid" in a class, in a neighborhood, in a club, or on a team.

Think of a time when you were the "new kid." How did you act? How did people treat you? Was it a good experience? List some words that describe how you felt.

Write a letter to a friend about your experience. Tell what happened in order. Include details about your feelings.

> This introduces the topic.

> This suggests ways to prewrite.

> This tells you your assignment: to write a personal narrative in the form of a letter.

Types of Writing Found on Tests

Types of Writing	Purpose	Clue Words in the Prompt
Narrative	to entertain, to tell a story	tell a story, tell about a time, tell what happened when
Informational	to explain or define	explain why, tell how, explain how you would
Persuasive	to persuade or convince	persuade, convince, tell why you think, explain why you would

Strategies for Interpreting a Prompt

Strategies	Applying the Strategies
Read the prompt.	• Read for a general sense of the topic and form.
Identify the topic, purpose, and form of your assignment.	• Locate clue words that tell you what you are supposed to do.
Restate your assignment.	• Silently tell yourself in your own words what your assignment is. For example, "I am supposed to write a speech to persuade my classmates to exercise" or "I am supposed to write an essay to explain how to use a simple machine."

Try This! Skim the writing prompts in this handbook (pages 8, 12, 16, 20, 24, 28, and 32). In your own words, explain what your assignment is for each prompt.

Managing Your Time

Writing with a time limit can be tricky. Most standardized tests allow you to prewrite, draft, and edit your work. You must complete all of these steps in a short time. Learning to manage your time can help you succeed on demand writing tests. These pie charts show how you might divide your time:

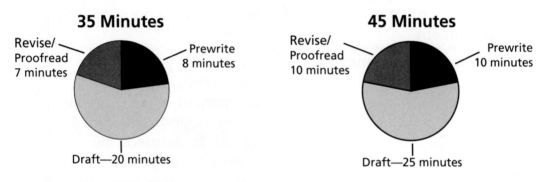

35 Minutes

Revise/Proofread 7 minutes

Prewrite 8 minutes

Draft—20 minutes

45 Minutes

Revise/Proofread 10 minutes

Prewrite 10 minutes

Draft—25 minutes

Strategies for Demand Writing	Applying the Strategies
Prewrite	• Jot down your topic and form. • List ideas, use graphic organizers, and brainstorm.
Draft	• Use your prewriting notes to write a draft. • Check to make sure you have done what the prompt asked you to do.
Revise/Proofread	• Add missing details. • Take out details that don't fit the topic. • Check your punctuation, capitalization, grammar, and spelling.

Writing Models

Story

A **story** has a setting, characters, and a plot. The characters and events in a **realistic story** are believable.

City Birds

Sandra pointed her camera at the very top of the tall silver skyscraper. She waited patiently. Her sister Ana was not so patient.

"I'm bored and I'm hot," said Ana.

"Shh. The falcon will come out today," said Sandra. "I know it will."

"Will not! I'm hungry. Let's go," wailed Ana.

Sandra ignored her. A peregrine falcon was supposed to be living at the top of this office building. Sandra was determined to get a picture of it.

Suddenly, Ana cried out, "Look! There it is!" Sandra turned around quickly. Ana was pointing across the street at a big pigeon.

"That's not a falcon," said Sandra. "Falcons are beautiful."

"I think that bird is beautiful."

The beginning introduces the characters and setting.

Dialogue shows what characters are like.

main character's goal

"It is not," Sandra shouted. "It's ugly! You can't tell the difference between a falcon and a pigeon."

Ana turned away and started to sniffle. Sandra was sorry she had gotten so angry. She went back to looking through her camera lens. The sisters sat back-to-back. They were as silent as two bookends.

events in the order in which they happen

Figurative language creates a vivid image.

Then Ana saw something. "Sandra," she whispered nervously.

"What is it?" snapped Sandra.

"Look up there, at that other building."

Ana pointed at the building across the street. Way up at the top, a small shadow swooped to a ledge. Sandra looked through her zoom lens. It was the falcon. She had been watching the wrong building.

"That's it!" she said. "Take a look." She handed her sister the camera. Ana looked through the lens.

"That's a beautiful bird, too," she said.

Sandra laughed. She let Ana push the button. It was going to be a beautiful picture.

ending

Folktale

Folktales are meant to be shared aloud. Many of them have elements of fantasy. Sometimes they teach a lesson, too.

The Clumsy Juggler

Hugo was a juggler. He was really good except for one little problem. He dropped everything. One day, he set up a sign. It said, "Hugo, the World's Best Juggler!" A crowd quickly gathered.

He dropped balls. "Boo," said the crowd. Then he dropped some sticks. "Boo, boo," said the crowd. Hugo was sad. He picked up his things and dumped them into a fountain. The moon felt sorry for Hugo. When Hugo fell asleep, the moon took out his paints.

The next day, Hugo tried again. Another crowd gathered. Hugo dropped everything again. The crowd laughed and gave him silver.

Hugo was confused. Then he looked at his sign. Now it said, "Hugo, the World's Clumsiest Juggler." Hugo looked up at the moon and smiled.

The title grabs the reader's attention.

repetition to create humor

The character and events are not realistic.

problem solved

Tall Tale

Tall tales use exaggeration and humor to tell unbelievable stories. They stretch the truth so far it breaks.

Glenda Garoo

The longest hair I ever knew was on Glenda Garoo. She could wrap it around her head eighty-two times. Long ago, she had regular hair like yours and mine. But then it grew.

You see, one day, Glenda's little boy, Hugh, fell down a well. Glenda stared down the well. She tried to think of a plan. She thought so hard that her brain fizzed with energy. That energy was so strong that it made her hair grow. The next thing you know, little Hugh was climbing up her hair. Glenda was so glad, she promised she'd never cut it. And she never did.

friendly, chatty language

unbelievable events

Exaggerated claims make the story humorous.

Descriptive Paragraph

A **descriptive paragraph** tells about one specific topic. The topic should be narrow enough to describe in a handful of sentences.

Grandfather's Bread

My grandfather's bread is both delicious to eat and gorgeous to look at. He brings a new loaf every Saturday. You can smell the warm bread even before he walks in. The dough is always twisted like a lock of braided hair. He paints the top with egg to make it dark mahogany brown. Then he sprinkles it with tasty sesame seeds. It looks almost too good to eat, but we always do. The crust is crisp and crunchy. The inside is soft, warm, and airy.

title

topic sentence

The writer uses details that apply to the senses: sight, hearing, smell, touch, and taste.

Descriptive Essay

You can describe a more complicated subject in a **descriptive essay.** Each paragraph in a descriptive essay focuses on one part of the whole picture. One way to arrange your ideas is to use spatial order—that is, you might describe your subject from top to bottom, from left to right, or from the middle out.

A Spanish American Street Fair

Last week, our block was closed off for a street fair. Spanish and American flags hung on all the telephone poles, and red and yellow streamers decorated every booth.

The first booths on the block sold Spanish American food. One booth sold spicy paella from a giant pan. It is made of rice, mussels, shrimp, and squid. At the next booth, you could smell empanadas, which are made of dough that is filled with beef or fish. Other booths sold gazpacho, a cold tomato soup.

The next booths tempted people to play games to win giant stuffed animals. One game booth was for throwing balls at milk bottles. Another game booth was for squirting water pistols into balloons.

In the middle of the block, a band platform was set up. Musicians played Spanish music on accordions and guitars all day long. Then some dancers performed a flamenco dance. This is a dance with lots of quick, clicking steps.

The introduction sets the scene.

explanation of unusual terms

The writer starts a new paragraph for each new subject.

spatial organization

The other half of the block was set up for selling things. Some things were everyday items, like pillows, T-shirts, and books. There were also some unusual items made in Spain. You could buy painted plates, carved leather bags, and beautiful beaded jewelry.

At the very end of the block sat a little Ferris wheel. It wasn't very high, but from the top you could see the whole scene perfectly. Our block was a blur of people, banners, music, and booths. What a party!

The conclusion gives the overall impression.

Character Sketch

When you want to describe a person, you can write a **character sketch.** You can tell your reader a lot about someone in just a few words, including how your subject looks, sounds, and acts.

Ms. Tuva is the checker at our corner grocery store. When you first see her, she looks sad. Her eyes are dark and always half-closed. Her face is very still. But when she starts talking, you can tell she's really friendly. Her voice is high, like a parakeet's. Every sentence is a song. She chatters about school, her family, and the weather. Her face never changes, but she sounds very excited. When you wave good-bye, she lifts her hand halfway and jiggles it a little. That's about as dramatic as Ms. Tuva gets.

The writer uses details that appeal to the senses.

figurative language

vivid verb

Response to Literature

In a response to literature, the writer presents his or her thoughts about a work of literature. The writer may focus on one or more aspects of the work—for example, one or more of the characters, events from the plot, or the theme of the story. The writer also includes details from the book to support his or her opinions and ideas.

The Island of the Blue Dolphins
by Scott O'Dell

The Island of the Blue Dolphins by Scott O'Dell tells the story of a twelve-year-old Native American girl, Karana, and how she survives alone on an island for many years. Karana shows her bravery and intelligence throughout this amazing story. The most incredible thing about the book is that it is based on the adventures of a real girl.

At the beginning of the story, Karana and her younger brother, Ramo, live with their father, who is the chief of the people of the island of Ghalas-At. Their father is killed in a fight when a ship of Aleuts hunting sea otters comes to the island. Soon, another ship comes to rescue the people of the island from a terrible hurricane that is headed their way.

Karana is on the deck of the rescue ship when she sees that Ramo has been left behind on the island. At this moment, Karana first shows her courage. She jumps from the ship and swims ashore to save her younger brother. The ship leaves, abandoning the two of them on their island home.

The introduction tells the title and author and states the problem that the main character faces.

The writer introduces the reader to the setting and background of the story.

The writer describes the event that sparks the story and lets the reader know how he feels about the main character.

Soon Karana's brother is killed by wild dogs on the island. Karana is alone now and must show even more courage to survive. She must hunt for her food, make clothing for herself, and find shelter to protect herself. She learns to fight the wild dogs. She even catches and trains the leader of the pack! Eventually, Karana herself brings about her biggest challenge when she decides to ride the giant waves to reach another island.

When a ship comes back to the island eighteen years later, Karana has grown into an extraordinary woman. She has become stronger and wiser with each new challenge. She has learned to accept her special place in the world and to love the simple pleasures of life.

Everyone who reads this book is sure to admire Karana. Anyone who can survive such difficult challenges for so long and make them into something positive has a lesson to teach everyone. I learned a lot from reading Karana's story, and I'm sure you will, too!

The writer describes the difficult things the main character must do to survive. These details help explain why the writer admires the main character.

The writer describes how the main character changes in response to her challenges.

The closing summarizes why the author admires the main character and why others will enjoy reading the book.

Summary

You can write a **summary** to help you remember something you have read or seen. You may also be asked to write a summary to show that you understand something you have read. A summary tells about main events or ideas. If you are summarizing a story, tell about the beginning, the middle, and the ending. If you are summarizing nonfiction, tell about the main ideas. Here are a nonfiction article and a student's summary of the article.

Voting Rights—The Road to Equality

sample source

Throughout most of American history, women did not enjoy the same rights as men. They could not own land. They could not make decisions about how their children were to be educated. Most importantly, they could not vote.

In the 1820s and 1830s, a number of white women began protesting the inequalities of slavery. It was through this struggle for human rights that they began to see the more subtle inequalities in their own lives.

In 1848, a number of important women activists, including Elizabeth Cady Stanton and Lucretia Mott, organized a woman suffrage convention at Seneca Falls, New York.

The delegates to the convention issued a proclamation based on the Declaration of Independence. In the document they said that "all men and women are created equal." They demanded that women be given "all the rights and privileges which belong to them as citizens of the United States."

Winning these rights took longer than expected. During the 1890s, several of the new western states gave women the right to vote. Eventually, some of the eastern and midwestern states did likewise. However, women still could not vote in national elections. That right was finally won in 1920 when the Nineteenth Amendment to the Constitution was ratified. At last, the right to have a say in the way the country is governed applied to its male *and* female citizens.

American women have not always had equal rights. In the early 1800s, the fight against slavery made some of them realize that they, too, were being treated unfairly. In 1848, some women held a convention and demanded suffrage, or the right to vote. However, the process of gaining women's suffrage was gradual and was not complete until the Nineteenth Amendment was passed in 1920.

summary

The writer uses his or her own words.

Personal Narrative

You can write about something that really happened to you in a **personal narrative**. Choose a memorable event and tell how you felt about it. Tell the beginning, middle, and ending of your story.

My pen pal, Tami, changed my life forever. I wrote her a letter when I was sad. I told her about the big race at school. I use a wheelchair, so I can't run. I told Tami how left out I felt.

She wrote back right away. She told me about the Special Olympics. It's a great organization for people who are challenged.

I called our local chapter. They hold wheelchair races. I was so excited that I entered right away. I wrote Tami a letter about my very first race. I think everybody should have a pen pal like Tami.

first-person pronouns (*my* and *I*)

details in time order

The ending tells how the writer feels

Paragraph of Information

An **information paragraph** tells the reader about one specific topic. You can write about a topic you know well, or you can research an interesting subject. The paragraph may include opinions if they are supported by facts.

The Library of Congress is the world's largest national library. It has more than 97 million items, including books, pamphlets, maps, photographs, and recordings. It has works in more than 450 languages. One way that the library gets books is through the United States copyright laws. Every work that is copyrighted must be submitted to the Library of Congress. Therefore, if you ever apply for a copyright, your manuscript will be on file in one of the most amazing libraries in the world.

The topic sentence states the main idea.

supporting details

The conclusion may include an opinion.

How-to Paragraph

A **how-to paragraph** is a perfect way to give a quick set of directions or some helpful advice. Clear writing will help a reader follow your advice, so avoid wordy and confusing sentences.

How to Improve Your Soccer Kick

Here are a few tricks that will help you shoot goals in soccer. Remember that the object of the game is to score. If you get a chance, take it. Look at the center of the ball when you kick it. Watch your foot hit the ball. Then follow through with your leg and your eyes. Put as much of your weight into the shot as you can without losing your balance. The best shooters are almost entirely off the ground when they kick. With a little practice, you'll be kicking better than ever.

The first sentence gets the reader's attention.

clear, direct instructions

Imperative sentences give directions.

How-to Essay

You can tell a reader how to follow a series of directions in a **how-to essay.** The reader has to be able to follow along easily, so the order of your steps is important.

A Personal Paper Doll

You can be a real doll! It's easy. Just follow these steps.

First, ask a friend to take several pictures of you. Stand in front of something blank, like a white wall. Make sure your feet are in the shot.

After you get the film developed, choose your favorite picture, and have it enlarged to about 8 inches high.

Next, glue your picture onto heavy cardboard. When the glue is dry, cut out your picture. Use a lump of clay to make a base, and set your picture in it.

You can now use cloth, paper, and glitter to dress up your doll. Make clothes, eyeglasses, hats, or shoes.

A personal paper doll makes an enjoyable toy or a good gift. It's an easy and amusing project for any time of year.

The writer puts the steps in logical order.

The conclusion tells why the activity is worthwhile.

Essay of Comparison and Contrast

When you write an **essay of comparison and contrast**, you explain how two things are similar and different. You can make it easy for your reader to understand your ideas by presenting your main points in a logical order. Start by telling how the two things are alike. Then tell how they differ. Be sure to include transition words to help make similarities and differences clear.

Cats or Dogs?

Imagine that your parents finally have agreed to bring a pet into the family. Your sister or brother wants a cat, but you want a dog. Your mom says that it has to be a family decision. Dogs and cats are alike in some ways and different in others. Here are some facts that may help you make the choice.

Both cats and dogs require special care. They must be fed regularly with healthful pet food. Both kinds of pets also need checkups with a veterinarian. Cats and dogs should be groomed regularly, especially if they have long hair. Exercise is important for pets, too. Before choosing a pet, remember that you will need to spend time and money on either a cat or a dog.

The introduction grabs the reader's attention.

Here's the main idea of the essay.

This paragraph tells how dogs and cats are alike.

The writer uses a variety of short and long sentences.

Choosing between a cat and a dog may depend on certain differences between these animals. Many dogs are playful and friendly, so they make good pals. They love to go outside, run in the park, or play games with their owners. Cats, on the other hand, are more independent and usually stay indoors. They enjoy and return affection in a quieter way. Whereas dogs can be taught to stay, sit, and roll over, cats are more difficult to train.

Whether your new pet barks or meows, it will be an important part of your family. Treat your pet well, and it will give you many happy moments.

This paragraph tells how dogs and cats are different.

"Cats, on the other hand" makes the transition.

The conclusion wraps up the essay in an interesting way.

Essay That Explains

In an **essay that explains,** a writer tells or describes why or how something happens. Science and social studies often involve writing an essay that explains.

When you write to explain, you must write clearly, precisely, and completely. For example, if you are writing about a science experiment, start by telling your reader the purpose of your experiment. Describe the materials you used and the steps of your experiment. Discuss what you observed and the conclusions you drew. Include a title that asks the key question your experiment tried to answer.

Can Goldfish Be Trained?

One day as I sat watching my pet goldfish swim around in the goldfish bowl, I came up with the idea that maybe a goldfish could be trained like a pet dog. I decided to conduct an experiment to test my hypothesis that it is possible to train a goldfish.

First, I assembled the materials for my experiment. I needed only the goldfish bowl, the goldfish, and goldfish food.

Next, I decided on a method to test my hypothesis. Here's what I did. Each time I fed the fish, I tapped on the bowl before I put the food in the water. I watched to see if the fish would come to the top of the water when I tapped.

The title asks the question that the experiment tried to answer.

The writer begins with an interesting idea.

Each paragraph focuses on one stage of the experiment.

Time-order words show sequence.

The method of the experiment is clearly stated.

I tapped on the bowl before each feeding for three weeks. For the first week, the fish ignored my tapping. It came to the surface only when I actually put food in the bowl.

On day 8, I finally saw a change. For the first time, the fish came to the top of the bowl as soon as I tapped. Over the next two weeks, more and more often the fish came to the top as soon as I tapped on the bowl.

Now, after 21 days, the fish always comes to the top of the bowl as soon as I tap. Even if I do not feed it right away, it still comes to the top. This experiment proves that goldfish can be trained to respond to a simple stimulus.

Observations are presented precisely.

Numbers help make the results and order of events clear.

The conclusion is based on the results of the experiment and is clearly stated.

News Story:
Interview Techniques

An audience reads a news story to find out current information. The story can answer the questions *who, what, when, where, why,* and *how.* One good way to find information for a news story is to **interview** somebody knowledgeable. Try these hints to become an expert interviewer:

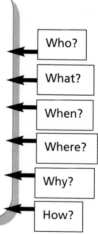

- Begin by writing the subject's name at the top of your page. Then list the facts you already know.

- Write a list of questions *before* you interview.

- Take notes while you talk. You can also tape-record your interview, but get the subject's permission first.

- Listen to your subject's responses. These will often make you think of more questions.

Simon Levy, the winner of the Video Showdown

1. Against whom did you play? ← Who?

2. What games did you play? ← What?

3. When did you first start playing? ← When?

4. Where was the contest held? ← Where?

5. Why do you think you won? ← Why?

6. How did you learn to play? ← How?

News Story

A **news story** has a headline, a lead paragraph, and a body. The lead paragraph introduces the topic. The body gives the rest of the information about the current event.

Simon Levy Wins Video Duel

Simon Levy won yesterday's Video Showdown at Arcadia, the new game arcade. The contest attracted fifty-four players. Simon played forty rounds to win the grand prize: a one-month free pass to Arcadia.

Levy attends fifth grade at Bowman Elementary School. He started playing video games when he was four. His older brother coached him.

Levy was modest about his victory. "I got lucky in the last round," he said. "Star Quest was selected for the final. That's my best game."

Alisha Jackson, the runner-up, said that it took more than luck. "This guy is amazing," she said.

The owner of Arcadia says she plans to have another Video Showdown next year.

The headline uses strong words to capture the reader's attention.

Lead tells *who, what, where,* and *when.*

body

Research Report: Note Taking

Note taking can help you remember what you learn from listening in class or from reading. Taking good notes can save time when you write a paper or study for a test. These tips can help you when you are taking notes:

- Include important words or phrases.

- Define new terms.

- Use abbreviations that make sense to you.

- Include the source of the information so that you can go back to it if necessary.

Carnivorous Plants

<u>Carnivorous</u> means "flesh-eating."

Carnivorous plants

– need nitrogen

– live in wetlands (no nitrogen)

– get nitrogen from insects they trap and eat

<u>Plants of the World</u>, J. Smith, 2003, p. 93

Write the name of the topic at the top of the card.

important details

source

Research Report: Outline

An **outline** can help you organize information for a research report. An outline uses Roman numerals for topics, capital letters for subtopics, and numbers for details. You should include at least two subtopics for every topic.

Carnivorous Plants

I. **Why carnivorous plants eat insects**   ← main topic
   A. They need nitrogen.
   B. Wetlands have very little nitrogen.   ← two or more subtopics for each topic
   C. Insects contain nitrogen.

II. **Kinds of carnivorous plants**
   A. Plants that move
      1. Venus's-flytrap   ← details
      2. Bladderworts
   B. Plants that do not move
      1. Pitcher plants
      2. Butterworts

III. **Why some carnivorous plants are becoming rare**
   A. Wetlands are decreasing.
   B. The plants can't survive in other areas.

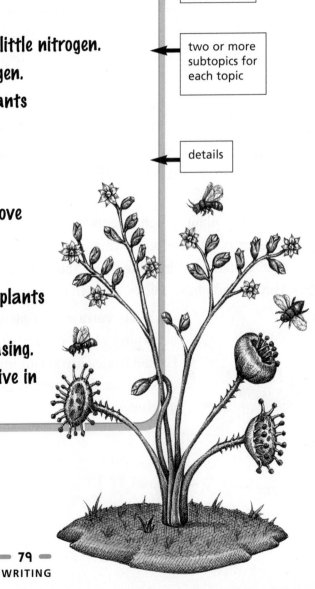

Research Report

A **research report** gives information about a topic. Use a variety of sources to find information. Remember to explain unfamiliar terms.

Carnivorous Plants

title

Plants that eat insects are called <u>carnivorous</u>. All plants need nitrogen to survive. Most carnivorous plants live in wetland areas. The soil there has very little nitrogen. Carnivorous plants get their nitrogen by eating insects.

explanation of the term *carnivorous*

Some carnivorous plants move to catch their prey. The Venus's-flytrap can shut its leaves around an insect. The two leaves snap together like a clam. Bladderworts use water pressure to trap underwater insects.

topic sentences followed by supporting details

Other plants catch insects without moving. Pitcher plants use pitfall traps. Insects are attracted to the plant, fall into the pool, and drown. Butterworts have sticky parts that act like flypaper.

facts presented in a logical order

Many carnivorous plants are becoming rare. Wetland areas in the United States are shrinking. Without these areas, carnivorous plants will not survive.

Forms

Forms require neat and careful writing. You may need to fill out forms to join clubs, to get a library card, or to buy merchandise from catalogs or the Internet. Read the form before you start filling it out.

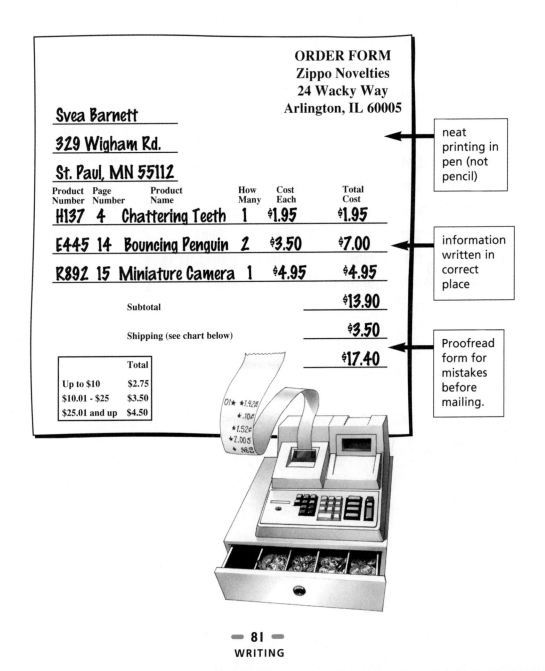

ORDER FORM
Zippo Novelties
24 Wacky Way
Arlington, IL 60005

Svea Barnett

329 Wigham Rd.

St. Paul, MN 55112

Product Number	Page Number	Product Name	How Many	Cost Each	Total Cost
H137	4	Chattering Teeth	1	$1.95	$1.95
E445	14	Bouncing Penguin	2	$3.50	$7.00
R892	15	Miniature Camera	1	$4.95	$4.95

Subtotal $13.90

Shipping (see chart below) $3.50

$17.40

	Total
Up to $10	$2.75
$10.01 - $25	$3.50
$25.01 and up	$4.50

neat printing in pen (not pencil)

information written in correct place

Proofread form for mistakes before mailing.

Persuasive Paragraph

A **persuasive paragraph** presents a short, clear argument. The writer tries to convince an audience that an opinion is correct. Facts and reasons are used to support the argument.

> I think that the Emerson High School pool should be open at night for our community. There is no public pool in town. The high school swim team doesn't use the pool after six o'clock. The pool could be open every night until nine. Everyone would have a chance to use the pool, including students who are not yet in high school. The school is already open for night classes. The only additional expenses would be a lifeguard and a security person, and I think that their fees could be paid for by community fund-raising. It is a shame to leave this beautiful pool unused.

thesis statement

Be sure to give good reasons that support your opinion.

Persuasive Essay

You may want to write a **persuasive essay** when you have a major point to make. Begin with a clear thesis statement. Each paragraph can offer a different reason to support your opinion.

I think that commercials should be banned from Saturday-morning television. It is unfair to expose children to advertising. The ads on Saturday are the worst.

Little children do not have critical abilities. They believe everything they see. Right now, they see a lot of ads. In fact, the average American sees about 3,000 ads every day.

The commercials on Saturday mornings are designed by adults to make children want things. It is not surprising that they work. Adults know how to make products look irresistible to children. This is not fair.

Teachers can help. They can use class time to teach children how to see through ads. That way, children will be prepared to resist the 125 ads they see every hour on Saturdays.

thesis statement

supporting ideas

negatives used to emphasize points

Book Review

How can you share your opinion of a book? A **book review** tells how a reader feels about a book. The reader discusses details from the book that support his or her opinion.

<u>The House of Dies Drear</u> by Virginia Hamilton is an exciting story. I never knew what was going to happen next. I liked it because it was so unpredictable.

It tells the story of Thomas Small and his family. They move into an old house that was once a station on the Underground Railroad. The house is supposed to be haunted by the ghosts of Dies Drear and two slaves who were murdered.

I thought the book was going to be a typical ghost story. Then a mysterious character named Mr. Pluto shows up. He wants to protect the historic house from greedy neighbors. They want to steal its treasures.

Anyone who likes a suspenseful story will like this book. It also has a lot of interesting information about life in America before the Civil War. I can't wait to read the sequel, <u>The Mystery of Drear House</u>.

name of book underlined; author identified

The writer supports his or her opinion with details from book.

recommendation

Movie Review

Reviewers share their opinions with readers. A **movie review** or **TV review** follows the same rules as a book review. A good review tells an audience what to expect without giving everything away.

Even though it was made in 1933, <u>King Kong</u> is an electrifying movie. It doesn't seem old-fashioned at all. I don't usually like black-and-white movies, but I loved this one.

> title of movie underlined

> opinions

Some scientists discover Kong on a remote island. They capture him and bring him to New York City. Of course, they can't keep him tied up for long.

The acting is very believable—especially that of Kong! The special effects are so convincing that I forgot Kong was just a model. Sometimes the movie looks like a documentary.

The final scene is the most famous. Kong climbs to the top of the Empire State Building. It is a very exciting climax. I have my doubts about the ending, though. I wish the writers had found a way to make it happier. Still, this movie is certainly worth seeing.

This movie was filled with suspense.

Play

Plays are written to be acted out. Dialogue, or the words the characters say, tells the story. Stage directions are written in parentheses. They tell a reader about the character's actions and emotions.

Only Kidding

Characters

MARIE, a practical joker

JODI, Marie's friend

GLENN, a new student

(Jodi and Marie are eating lunch in the school cafeteria.)

JODI: Hey, look. There's Glenn.

MARIE: Let's play a joke on him, OK?

JODI: Sure. Hey, Glenn, come here.

(Glenn sits down.)

GLENN: Hi, Marie. Hi, Jodi.

MARIE: Mom always makes me a peanut butter sandwich, and I hate peanut butter.

GLENN: I have tomato and cheese.

MARIE: That sounds good. You want to trade?

GLENN: (hesitantly) I guess so.

cast list

setting

Character names show who is talking.

(Glenn bites into the sandwich and looks
amazed. Marie and Jodi laugh.)

Stage
directions
show action.

GLENN: Yuck! This isn't peanut butter. It's
tuna fish!

JODI: You should see your face!

GLENN: (gasping) I'm allergic . . . to . . . tuna
fish . . . . (He faints.)

MARIE: (nervously) Oh, no! Now look what
you've done!

vivid adverbs
used to
show how a
line should
be said

JODI: Me? It was you who did it!

MARIE: What are we gonna do?

(Glenn sits up.)

GLENN: (cheerfully) Only kidding.
I love tuna fish. But that'll teach you to
play silly tricks!

Ending wraps
up the story.

Charts

A **chart** is a visual way of showing a lot of information. Charts are set up in rows and columns. To find the information you need, you read across rows and down columns. Titles and headings help you locate information on charts. Most word processing programs include easy ways to create professional-looking charts. When you create a chart, the following tips will be helpful:

- First, gather all the information you want to include.
- Think about the best way to organize the information.
- Give your chart a title so the reader knows what it is about.

Animal Names			
Animal	Male	Female	Young
bear	boar	sow	cub
deer	buck	doe	fawn
fox	dog	vixen	cub
rabbit	buck	doe	bunny
turkey	tom	hen	poult

title ← (Animal Names)

headings ← (Animal | Male | Female | Young)

Graphs

A **graph** is a special kind of chart. We use graphs to compare information about numbers. Two useful kinds of graphs are bar graphs and line graphs.

A **bar graph** uses bars to represent numbers. The bars can run from side to side, or they can run up and down. To read a bar graph, find the number where each bar stops. That location tells you what number each bar represents.

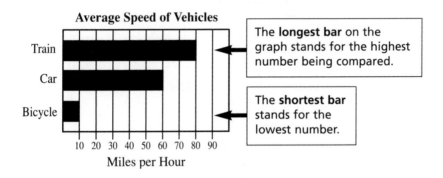

Average Speed of Vehicles

The **longest bar** on the graph stands for the highest number being compared.

The **shortest bar** stands for the lowest number.

A **line graph** uses points on a line to represent numbers. To read a line graph, find the height of each point on the line.

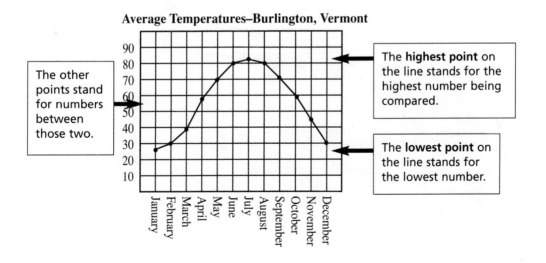

Average Temperatures–Burlington, Vermont

The other points stand for numbers between those two.

The **highest point** on the line stands for the highest number being compared.

The **lowest point** on the line stands for the lowest number.

Diagrams

A **diagram** is a visual way of organizing information. Sometimes a diagram uses graphics and words to classify or categorize. You can use a Venn diagram to show how things are alike and different. The words in the nonintersecting parts of the circles show differences. The words in the part that intersects tell about similarities.

Major Exports

Coal
Citrus Fruits
Coffee

Tea
Corn
Beef

Gold
Iron
Tin

Mozambique   Zimbabwe

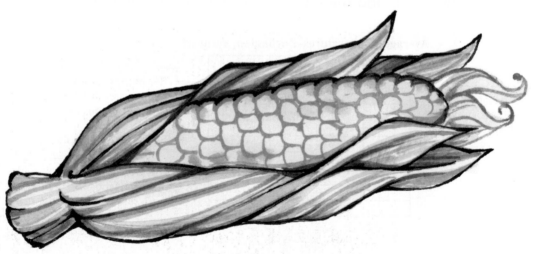

Grammar, Usage and Mechanics

DECLARATIVE AND INTERROGATIVE SENTENCES

- A **sentence** is a group of words that expresses a complete thought.
- A **declarative sentence** is a statement and ends with a period.
- An **interrogative sentence** is a question and ends with a question mark.

Identify each group of words as a complete sentence or a sentence fragment. Rewrite the sentence fragments, adding words to make them complete sentences.

1. **Glanced up at the window.**
2. **The boys saw a bird.**
3. **Was it sitting on a branch?**
4. **How did Lucette?**
5. **Where was?**

Write each sentence correctly, using a capital letter and an end mark. Then write *declarative* or *interrogative* to tell what kind of sentence it is.

6. **everyone began to applaud**
7. **what was the big fuss**
8. **has anyone seen Lucette**
9. **the bird flew from tree to tree**

DECLARATIVE AND INTERROGATIVE SENTENCES

Read the numbered word groups on the poster. Write each word group. Underline each word group that is a complete sentence. Circle each word group that is not a complete sentence.

$25 REWARD!

1. Have you seen a large green bird with a blue-and-red head lately?
2. My name is Bolivia Golding.
3. Address—Dogleg Lane
4. Parrot—missing since Thursday
5. Name—Lucette
6. Favorite food—fruit

7.–10. Rewrite the circled items on Bolivia's notice. Add words to make each word group a complete sentence. Then write whether each sentence is declarative or interrogative.

CUMULATIVE REVIEW

Read each group of words. Write which groups are sentences and which are not sentences.

1. Talk with their mouths full of food.
2. Are some burgers made with turkey?
3. The public library shows free movies.
4. Swimming in the pool.
5. Can we teach Lucette new words?

Write the sentences correctly, using capital letters and end marks. Then identify each sentence as declarative or interrogative.

6. are the boys good swimmers
7. there is a waiting period for a pool card
8. do you think Bolivia can swim
9. the boys must sneak out of the house
10. how long will Bolivia visit
11. Where did you find Lucette
12. lucette was in that tree

IMPERATIVE AND EXCLAMATORY SENTENCES

Rewrite each sentence to make it an imperative sentence with the subject *you* understood. Remember to capitalize and punctuate each sentence correctly.

1. I want you to sit on the rock.
2. I want you to listen carefully.
3. I want you to look with your ears.
4. I do not want you to move.
5. I want you to tell what you see.

Write the sentences correctly, using capital letters and end marks. Then write whether the sentence is imperative or exclamatory.

6. how soft the brook sounds
7. do not wade into the river now
8. what lovely roses those are
9. how beautiful that bird is
10. put down your bow
11. describe this place

IMPERATIVE AND EXCLAMATORY SENTENCES

1.–6. Read the page from a zoo brochure below. Write which are the imperative sentences and which are the exclamatory sentences.

SENSES IN THE WILD

What keen eyes tigers have!

Imagine being able to see at night.

Look at this elephant's trunk.

What an amazing sense of smell sharks have!

Please don't feed the monkeys.

What excellent hearing bats have!

7.–12. Choose six of your favorite animals. Write one exclamatory sentence and one imperative sentence about each animal. You may use the brochure sentences as models.

CUMULATIVE REVIEW

Read the sentences below. Write what each sentence is: *declarative,*
interrogative, imperative, or *exclamatory.*

1. Can he hear those sounds?

2. His eyes can see very little.

3. Did his uncle discover that?

4. What amazing hearing he has!

5. His hearing makes up for his bad eyes.

Rewrite the sentences correctly, using capital letters and end marks.

6. the forest is full of many different sounds

7. how sensitive the boy's hearing is

8. he cannot see his uncle's fingers

9. try to hear a hummingbird

10. how can he tell a hummingbird just by its sound

11. she spoke in a slow voice

12. who will begin

COMPLETE AND SIMPLE SUBJECTS

- Every sentence is made up of two parts, a subject and a predicate. The **subject** names the person or thing the sentence is about. The **predicate** tells what the subject is or does.
- The **complete subject** includes all the words that name the person or thing the sentence is about. The **simple subject** is the main word or words in the complete subject.

Write each of the following sentences. Draw one line under the complete subject, and draw two lines under the predicate.

1. Fourth Brother talked with Mary about the cat named Rita.
2. The children worried about Rita's safety.
3. Mary remembered the juggling act in China.
4. Three plates spun at the ends of three chopsticks.
5. The Yangs' piano had not been tuned for some time.

Read each of the following sentences. Identify the complete subject and the simple subject.

6. Piles of sheet music lay on the sofa and on the floor.
7. A clatter of falling music stands interrupted Mrs. Hanson.
8. Mother played a fast scale across the keyboard.
9. The look on Holly's face was uncomfortable.
10. Holly's technique was fairly good.

11.–12. Choose two of the sentences from 6 through 10 above. Rewrite them, substituting a new complete subject for the original one in each sentence.

COMPLETE AND SIMPLE SUBJECTS

Write each sentence below. Underline the complete subject. Circle the simple subject.

1. The woodwind section of an orchestra often includes eight instruments.

2. The piccolo has the highest range.

3. A flute produces silvery, velvety tones.

4. The sound of an oboe is sharp and sad.

5. Two small pieces of cane are in the mouthpiece of the English horn.

6. The clarinet has quite a wide range of pitches.

7. The range of the contrabassoon corresponds to that of the cello.

8. The bassoon is another woodwind instrument.

9.–12. Mary has a lot of different feelings. Write sentences that express Mary's feelings about each of the following: Mother, Fourth Brother, Holly, and the kitten Rita. Underline the complete subject of each sentence you write. Circle the simple subject.

CUMULATIVE REVIEW

Read the following sentences. Identify the complete subject and simple subject in each sentence.

1. Wolfgang Amadeus Mozart lived in the eighteenth century.
2. Mozart was one of the world's greatest composers.
3. Young Wolfgang played duets with his sister.
4. His father was a musician in Salzburg, Austria.
5. The talented child was a remarkable pianist by the age of three!

Write the sentences correctly, using capital letters and end marks. Then identify each sentence as declarative, interrogative, imperative, or exclamatory.

6. how many ten-year-old children have composed symphonies
7. what an amazing talent Mozart had
8. can you hum any of his famous melodies
9. play this piece on the piano for me
10. the Chang family liked to play music by Mozart

COMPLETE AND SIMPLE PREDICATES

- The **complete predicate** includes all the words that tell what the subject of the sentence is or does.
- The **simple predicate** is the main word or words in the complete predicate.

Read each sentence below. Identify the complete predicate and the simple predicate.

1. **Rosa Lee Parks lived in Alabama.**
2. **She became famous in 1955.**
3. **She rode on a bus one day in the city of Montgomery.**
4. **Mrs. Parks fought for her rights.**
5. **She claimed her seat on the bus.**
6. **Mrs. Parks showed a great deal of courage.**

Rewrite each sentence. Add a simple predicate to replace the blank.

7. **Many people _____ to Mrs. Parks for advice.**
8. **She _____ every letter.**
9. **Mrs. Parks _____ a very wise person.**
10. **Children _____ Mrs. Parks about many things.**
11. **Mrs. Parks _____ learning about life.**
12. **Mrs. Parks _____ her experiences with others.**

COMPLETE AND SIMPLE PREDICATES

A student wrote these notes for a book report about *Dear Mrs. Parks*.
Use the notes to write complete sentences. In your sentences,
underline each simple predicate.

1. Rosa Parks-book, *Dear Mrs. Parks*
2. Gregory J. Reed—helped
3. Book-short sections
4. Section-letter to Mrs. Parks
5. her reply to the letter
6. Mrs. Parks-very wise person
7. letters-her beliefs
8. encourages-be special
9. today-gives speeches
10. Civil Rights movement-influence

CUMULATIVE REVIEW

Write the sentences. Draw a line between the complete subject and the complete predicate in each sentence.

1. Everyone in Tina's class interviewed an older person.
2. Tina talked with her father's aunt.
3. Her great-aunt Sophia is seventy-three years old.
4. She came to the United States from Greece as a young girl.

Rewrite the following sentences. Correct errors in capitalization and punctuation. Then write whether each sentence is declarative, interrogative, imperative, or exclamatory.

5. look at this picture of Athens
6. have you been to Greece
7. how tall those columns are
8. that building is the Parthenon
9. Greece has many olive trees
10. would you like to visit Greece

Read each of the following sentences. Identify the complete predicate and the simple predicate.

11. Her stories about Greece in the old days were interesting.
12. Sophia went to school in a small fishing village.
13. Most people in the village were very poor.
14. Sophia's parents brought her to the United States in 1946.

COMPOUND SUBJECTS AND PREDICATES

Write each sentence. Underline the compound subject. Circle the conjunction that joins the subjects.

1. Mick and Phoebe liked riding their bikes together.
2. Phoebe and her friends played soccer last Thursday.
3. Pop, Mom, and Phoebe planned to go to the beach.
4. Swimming or diving is a lot of fun.
5. Blotches, blisters, or peeling may result from a bad sunburn.

Write each sentence. Underline the compound predicate. Circle the conjunction that joins the predicates.

6. Mrs. Berryhill called Phoebe to the office and spoke to her.
7. The teacher smiled and introduced another woman to Phoebe.
8. The woman explained the reasons for the assembly and invited Phoebe to speak.
9. Phoebe stood up, took her hand away, and refused the invitation.
10. Phoebe left the room but later changed her mind.

COMPOUND SUBJECTS AND PREDICATES

Combine each pair of sentences into one sentence with a compound subject or a compound predicate.

1. Phoebe watched the Three Stooges. Mick watched the Three Stooges.

2. Phoebe stood. Phoebe walked to the microphone.

Use the following compound subjects or compound predicates to write complete sentences.

3. Fog, rain, and snow (subject)

4. Windshield wipers and headlights (subject)

5. Drivers and passengers (subject)

6. An accident or an injury (subject)

7. use proper signal lights and make turns slowly (predicate)

8. slow down at intersections, watch for pedestrians, and obey traffic signals (predicate)

9. do stupid things but "luck out" (predicate)

10. take precautions and use common sense (predicate)

CUMULATIVE REVIEW

Choose the best way to rewrite each underlined section. If the underlined section needs no change, write "No mistake."

(1) <u>there was a dangerous intersection near Phoebe's house?</u> Phoebe's father (2) <u>griped, grumbled, but complained</u> about it. The city installed a traffic signal, but some people ignored it. (3) <u>Common sense is needed on the road. Good judgment is needed on the road.</u> Drivers and passengers should wear seat belts. (4) <u>Smart pedestrians stop, look, and listen before crossing the road.</u>

1. A There was a dangerous intersection near Phoebe's house!

   B There was a dangerous intersection near Phoebe's house.

   C There was a dangerous intersection near Phoebe's house?

   D No mistake

2. F griped, grumbled, and complained

   G griped grumbled but complained

   H griped grumbled and complained

   J No mistake

3. A Common sense is needed on the road, but good judgment.

   B Common sense is needed and good judgment on the road.

   C Common sense and good judgment are needed on the road.

   D No mistake

4. F Smart pedestrians stop, look, or listen before crossing the road.

   G Smart pedestrians stop look, and listen before crossing the road.

   H smart pedestrians stop, look, but listen before crossing the road.

   J No mistake

SIMPLE AND COMPOUND SENTENCES

Write whether each sentence is *simple* or *compound.*

1. The second baseman rushed in, but the ball bounced off his glove.

2. Noise filled the stadium and drowned out the announcer's voice.

3. Clemente hit the ball, but the Mets committed an error.

Combine each pair of simple sentences to form a compound sentence. Be sure to use a comma and a conjunction (*and, or, but*).

4. He was up three more times. He could not get another hit.

5. Jon Matlack pitched the next day. Roberto's fans and teammates were nervous.

6. Roberto could stay in Puerto Rico. He could go to Nicaragua and help the earthquake survivors.

SIMPLE AND COMPOUND SENTENCES

Identify the type of error in each sentence.

1. A giant earthquake hit Nicaragua more than 6,000 people were killed.

2. Thousands were homeless, people needed food and water.

A journalist has made notes for an article about Roberto Clemente and has asked you to help write the article. Use one of the conjunctions from the box below to combine each pair of sentences.

and	but	or

3. A fourteen-year-old boy had lost his legs in an accident. He had no money for artificial limbs.

4. A Puerto Rican baseball team raised some money for the boy. Roberto contributed the rest.

5. A severe earthquake occurred in Nicaragua. More than 6,000 people were killed.

6. Was the boy alive? Had he been killed in the earthquake?

7. An airplane full of supplies took off. Roberto was on the plane.

8. The pilot tried to return to the airport. The plane crashed into the sea.

CUMULATIVE REVIEW

Write the following sentences. Underline the compound subject or compound predicate in each sentence. Circle the conjunction that joins the subjects or predicates.

1. Roberto was sick and had lost weight.

2. His teammates and his coach worried about him.

3. He had 93 hits but needed 25 more.

4. His family and his friends were not concerned.

Write whether each sentence is *declarative, interrogative, imperative,* or *exclamatory.*

5. The Clemente family went to the baseball game.

6. Did they all think Roberto would get a hit?

7. Don't forget napkins.

8. What a great game it was!

For each sentence below, specify the error. Then rewrite the sentence correctly.

9. A baseball player uses a bat a hockey player uses a hockey stick.

10. Baseball fans watch the games in warm weather football fans watch in cold weather.

11. Scores in baseball games can be low, scores in basketball can be very high.

12. My favorite sport is soccer, I want to go to the World Cup one day.

CLAUSES

- A **clause** is a group of words that has both a subject and a predicate.
- **Independent clauses** are clauses that can stand alone as sentences.
- **Dependent clauses** are clauses that cannot stand alone as sentences.
- A dependent clause often begins with a connecting word, such as *before, after, because, although, since,* or *when.*

Write the sentences. Each sentence has one or two clauses. Draw one line under the independent clauses and two lines under the dependent clauses.

1. Owen Zabriske was at bat in the eighth inning.
2. Fans filled the stadium before the game began.
3. After Owen hit the home run, the crowd stood up.
4. When Emma uncurled her fingers, they saw the ball in her hand.
5. When Emma looked up, she saw herself on the giant screen.

Rewrite each item, adding the kind of clause asked for in parentheses. Punctuate sentences correctly.

6. Although the guard tried to persuade Emma (independent)
7. We will give you this brand-new ball (dependent)
8. When the office door opened (independent)
9. Owen sat down (dependent)
10. Because the Bombers needed the equipment (independent)

CLAUSES

The story of Owen Zabriske's 3,000th hit and the deal he made to get the ball was reported on television news the next morning. Unfortunately, the newscaster's cue cards got mixed up. On each cue card is a clause. Rearrange the cue cards so that the story makes sense.

Because Owen wanted the ball

the ball was there.

When Emma looked under the seat,

it sailed into the stands.

When the security guards found the ball,

no one knew who had the ball.

After Owen hit the ball,

he gave Emma brand-new equipment for it.

Because of the confusion,

they asked Emma to give it to them.

CUMULATIVE REVIEW

Write each sentence. Underline the simple sentences that make up each compound sentence.

1. The guards came toward us, and we became scared.
2. We asked to stay in our seats, but the guards took us away.
3. Emma will stand firm, or she will give the guards the baseball.
4. Owen needed the baseball, and Emma traded it for lots of equipment.

Write each sentence. Use correct punctuation and capitalization. Identify whether each sentence has a *compound subject* or a *compound predicate.*

5. a puff of wind got under the baseball and sent it out of the playing field
6. emma and Michael watched it
7. the baseball bounced and rolled under the seats
8. emma and many other fans tried to find the baseball

Read each group of words below. Write whether each is a sentence or is not a sentence.

9. When the game started, the sun was in our faces.
10. After the trade had been made.
11. Before the game ended, the weather service had predicted high winds.
12. When Emma got home.

COMPLEX SENTENCES

Write each sentence. Identify whether it is simple or complex. If it is complex, draw one line under the independent clause and two lines under the dependent clause. Circle the connecting word.

1. When Dusty reaches the first road, the team roars over the pavement.

2. The sled goes too fast and skids sideways.

3. When does he return to the trail?

4. Dusty passes the last racer before he reaches the fourth road.

5. After he reaches the main trail, the hilly section of the race begins.

Rewrite each sentence by reversing the order of the independent and dependent clauses. Be sure to use the comma correctly.

6. The dogs run into two snowmobiles when the sled goes around a blind corner.

7. The dogs get tangled up in their lines before Dusty can get to them.

8. Dusty runs beside the sled if the hills are steep.

9. Dusty jumps from runner to runner when he rounds a tight corner.

COMPLEX SENTENCES

Write each sentence. Draw one line under the independent clause and two lines under the dependent clause in each sentence.

1. Dusty's fears grow when he spots moose tracks.

2. Because dogs look like wolves to a moose, the moose may attack a team.

3. A moose may kill several dogs before a musher frightens it off.

4. If Dusty sees a moose, he will stop.

Combine each pair of sentences into a complex sentence, using a connecting word from the box. Not all the words will be used. Add commas where needed.

after as because if when although before since until while

5. He saw the open meadow. Dusty breathed a sigh of relief.

6. Two dogs have splits in the webs of their toes. Dusty puts booties on their feet.

7. This task takes only five minutes. He expects to see another racer behind him.

8. At the Yentna River, Dusty does not need to yell orders. The dogs know the way.

9. The water heats. Dusty fills a cooler with 20 pounds of hamburger.

10. Dusty dishes up the dogs' meal. Twenty hungry eyes watch him.

CUMULATIVE REVIEW

Write each sentence. Underline the independent clause once. Underline the dependent clause twice.

1. When he ran last year's race, Dusty came in fourth.
2. Dusty got lost for four hours before he found the right trail.
3. This happened because his glasses became coated with ice.
4. Before they left for headquarters, he and his father put the dogs into their traveling pens.

Write the following sentences. Write whether each sentence is *simple* or *compound.* If it is compound, underline the independent clauses.

5. Dusty arrived at headquarters, and all his friends were there.
6. The racers picked numbers from a hat.
7. The numbers determine a racer's starting position.
8. Dusty was worried, but he picked a good number.

Combine each pair of simple sentences into a complex sentence. Use the connecting word in parentheses.

9. Dusty is worried. The lake ice might be too slick. (because)
10. He had to use his hook. It wouldn't be able to grab the ice. (if)
11. A moose could cause trouble. It might mistake the dogs for wolves. (because)
12. Dogs can choke themselves. They get tangled up in the lines. (if)

COMMON AND PROPER NOUNS; ABBREVIATIONS

- A **noun** names a person, a place, a thing, or an idea.
- A **common noun** names any person, place, thing, or idea and begins with a lowercase letter.
- A **proper noun** is the name or title of a specific person, place, or thing. Begin each important word of a proper noun with a capital letter.
- Some common and proper nouns are often abbreviated. Use a period after most abbreviations, except after the abbreviations of metric measures.
- Begin the abbreviation of a proper noun with a capital letter.

Write each sentence. Underline the common nouns. Circle the proper nouns. Don't forget abbreviations.

1. The city of Juneau gets more than 100 in., or 254 cm, of snow every year.

2. Juneau is the capital of Alaska.

3. Twelve mountains in Alaska are more than 15,000 ft. high.

4. The trail is only 5 ft. 6 in. wide here.

Rewrite the sentences with correct capitalization and punctuation. Underline the proper nouns in each sentence you write.

5. Alaska became the forty-ninth State on jan 3, 1959.

6. Tourist attractions there include denali national park.

7. This park surrounds Mt McKinley, the tallest peak in north america.

8. That mountain is 20,320 ft high.

COMMON AND PROPER NOUNS; ABBREVIATIONS

Rewrite the following press release with correct capitalization and punctuation.

(1) Nome, alaska. Mar 11.

(2) The winner of this year's Iditarod Trail sled dog Race is Mr Martin buser. (3) The race course runs for 1,100 mi from anchorage to Nome. (4) Buser finished the course in 9 days, 8 hr, and 31 min. (5) buser was awarded $50,000 in prize money and a truck valued at $38,000.

Rewrite the abbreviations correctly.

6. mt McKinley

7. jr Iditarod race

8. 1,049 mi

9. feb 3

10. 15 in

11. dr. Jones

12. 1st ave

13. 24 ft

CUMULATIVE REVIEW

Rewrite each sentence so that it is the type of sentence named in parentheses. You may have to drop, add, or change some words.

1. **Will you tell me your opinion about the sled race? (imperative)**
2. **The end of the race was exciting. (exclamatory)**
3. **Your seats near the finish line were good ones. (interrogative)**
4. **How happy the winner looked! (declarative)**

Combine each pair of sentences to make a complex sentence. Use the connecting word shown in parentheses.

5. **Onlookers were in suspense. They finally saw two dog teams come into view. (until)**
6. **The winner appeared. The spectators cheered. (when)**

Write a common noun and a proper noun for each type.

7. **Person**
8. **Place**
9. **Thing**

Write abbreviations for the words below.

10. **boulevard**
11. **Mister**
12. **millimeters**
13. **pounds**
14. **Doctor**
15. **Junior**

SINGULAR AND PLURAL NOUNS

Each sentence contains one or more nouns. Write each noun and its plural form.

1. I swam to the shore.
2. I took my brother to the beach.
3. I could see the moon in the sky.
4. Where will you sail the ship?
5. She borrowed my skirt.

Rewrite each sentence, using the correct plural form of the noun in parentheses.

6. Ramo searched for food among the (bush).
7. He picked (berry) and put them in his basket.
8. His sister gathered (seed) in a ravine.
9. The (wave) crashed against the shore.
10. (Patch) of seaweed covered the rocks.

SINGULAR AND PLURAL NOUNS

Look at each picture. Write the singular and plural forms of the person or thing you see.

1.

2.

3.

4.

5.

6.

7.

8.

9.–11. Choose three plural nouns from the list above. Write a sentence for each of the plural nouns.

CUMULATIVE REVIEW

Choose the best way to rewrite each underlined section. If the underlined section needs no change, write "No mistake."

(1) <u>The storm was strong, and ships came for the people.</u> The girls quickly packed (2) <u>a few itemes</u> in their baskets. Ramo helped carry a basket. (3) <u>He forgot his spear, he could not go back for it.</u> Everyone thought Ramo was aboard the large ship. (4) <u>When Karana got on the ship. Her brother was not on board.</u>

1. A The storm was strong ships came for people.

   B The storm was strong but ships came for the people.

   C The Storm was strong, and ships came for the people.

   D No mistake

2. F a few item

   G a few items

   H a few itemies

   J No mistake

3. A He forgot his spear he could not go back for it.

   B He forgot his spear. he could not go back for it

   C He forgot his spear, but he could not go back for it.

   D No mistake

4. F When Karana got on the ship, her brother was not on board.

   G Karana got on the ship when her brother was not on board.

   H When Karana got on the Ship her brother was not on board.

   J No mistake

POSSESSIVE NOUNS

- A **possessive noun** shows ownership.
- To form the possessive of most singular nouns, add an apostrophe and s ('s).
- To form the possessive of a plural noun that ends in s, add only an apostrophe ('). To form the possessive of a plural noun that does not end in s, add an apostrophe and an s ('s).

Write each sentence. Circle the singular possessive noun in each sentence.

1. The dog's actions were strange.
2. The animal's tail bent down, not up.
3. Jonathan's sister heard a rumble.
4. Jonathan knew that Moose's senses were sharp.
5. The earthquake's approach was sudden.

Write each sentence, using a plural possessive noun for the singular possessive noun.

6. The frog's croaking stopped.
7. The tree's branches bent in the wind.
8. Jonathan and Abby couldn't hear the magpie's cries.
9. The redwood's crashing frightened Jonathan.
10. The children needed their parent's protection.
11. Jonathan remembered his class's earthquake drills.

POSSESSIVE NOUNS

Write each sentence, using the correct possessive noun form. Then identify it as *singular* or *plural.*

1. (Jonathan) parents were happy to see the children.
2. The (parents) greatest worry was that the children might be injured.
3. It was an (hour) drive back to camp.
4. Abby and Jonathan were relieved to hear their (father) voice.
5. Abby walked into her (mother) arms.
6. The (children) experience was frightening.

Write a sentence that combines each pair of sentences into one sentence. Replace the underlined words with a possessive noun.

7. I saw a nest. The nest <u>belonged to a robin</u>.
8. The children rode home in a car. The car <u>belonged to their cousins</u>.
9. I borrowed a book. The book <u>belonged to Matthew</u>.
10. Jeannie bought a new shirt. It is just like the one <u>belonging to Anna</u>.

CUMULATIVE REVIEW

Write the correct singular or plural form that fits each sentence.

1. Jonathan catalogs his baseball (card, cards).
2. Abby's mother wears her seat (belt, belts).
3. The (road, roads) in the woods are winding.
4. Jonathan wants to see a forest (ranger, rangers).
5. Jonathan practices earthquake (drill, drills) at school.

Write whether each sentence is *simple* or *compound*.

6. Jonathan's hobby is reading.
7. Jonathan finishes a book, and he shares it with a friend.
8. Abby likes to listen to music.
9. This song is very popular now.
10. She would play it on her guitar, but she doesn't have the music.

Write each sentence, changing the underlined word to a singular or a plural possessive noun. The word in parentheses tells you which form to use.

11. The <u>Millers</u> new pet is a rabbit. (plural)
12. I like to watch <u>rabbits</u> noses twitch. (plural)
13. My <u>cats</u> name is Daisy. (singular)
14. My two <u>aunts</u> favorite animals are otters. (plural)
15. An otter shows affection by biting its <u>owners</u> ears. (singular)

PRONOUNS AND ANTECEDENTS

Write each sentence. Circle the pronoun. Underline the antecedent. Then write *singular* or *plural* to indicate the number.

1. The fires spread fast, and they were soon out of control.
2. The smoke was so thick that it blocked out the sun.
3. Lightning strikes were common, and they caused many fires.
4. One firefighter was so exhausted that she had to stop.
5. The burned area covered many acres; it was huge.
6. A firefighter drove to the entrance, but it was closed.

Rewrite each sentence, replacing the underlined word or words with a singular or plural pronoun.

7. The fire burned until rain put the fire out.
8. Can these trees be saved, or will the trees die?
9. The firefighters often worked until the firefighters were exhausted.
10. Sara saw a frightened deer, and she wanted to help the deer.

PRONOUNS AND ANTECEDENTS

These sentences form part of a news report about the fire. Rewrite each sentence by replacing the underlined word or words with a pronoun. Circle the antecedent of the pronoun you wrote. Write *singular* if the pronoun and antecedent are singular or *plural* if they are plural.

1. Forests need wildfires, but that summer there were too many <u>wildfires</u>.
2. The ranger said that <u>the ranger</u> was worried about the animals.
3. Winds spread the fires and fed <u>the fires</u> with fresh oxygen.
4. Observers said that <u>the observers</u> actually saw a boulder burst from the heat.
5. The Old Faithful Inn seemed to be in danger, but the fire passed <u>The Old Faithful Inn</u> by.
6. The pilot flew low because <u>the pilot</u> wanted to drive the buffalo away from the fire.

7.–10. Write four sentences of your own, using a pronoun and its antecedent.

CUMULATIVE REVIEW

Write each sentence, changing the word in parentheses to a singular or a plural possessive noun. Then identify each possessive noun you write as singular or plural.

1. Have you seen the (Warners) new camper?
2. (Lucy) automobile is parked in the lot.
3. The (pilot) favorite park is Yellowstone.
4. The two (brothers) luggage was left at the inn.

For each sentence, identify the simple predicate.

5. The captain spoke to the firefighters.
6. He wanted to encourage them.
7. The guests at the Old Faithful Inn left.
8. Everyone waited for the rains to come.

For each sentence, choose the pronoun in parentheses that agrees with its antecedent. Write *singular* if it is a singular pronoun or *plural* if it is a plural pronoun.

9. Lola and her parents have invited me to go with (them, him) on vacation.
10. Lola's mother will drive, and (they, she) told me the trip will take ten hours.
11. Driving in the mountains is difficult, and (it, they) takes skill.

SUBJECT AND OBJECT PRONOUNS

- A **subject pronoun** takes the place of a noun or nouns in the subject of a sentence. *I, he, she, we,* and *they* are subject pronouns. Always capitalize the pronoun *I*. In a compound subject, *I* always comes last.

- An **object pronoun** takes the place of a noun after an action verb or after a preposition, such as *about, at, from, to,* or *with*. The words *me, him, her, us,* and *them* are object pronouns. In a compound object, *me* always comes last.

- *You* and *it* can be subject or object pronouns.

Identify the subject pronoun in each sentence.

1. **We saw photos of a tsunami.**

2. **It was caused by an earthquake.**

3. **They can be very dangerous.**

4. **I like watching waves wash up on the beach.**

5. **Alberto and I are learning how to surf.**

Write each sentence, using a subject pronoun or an object pronoun for each blank.

6. **A ship can sink if waves dump enough water on ____.**

7. **Swimmers must watch for breakers that can swamp ____.**

8. **The lifeguard warned Millie and ____ of the danger.**

9. **The waves washed over ____.**

10. **____ helped Timmy and me with our sand castle.**

SUBJECT AND OBJECT PRONOUNS

Read the sentences in the pictures. Identify each pronoun.

1.

"Are you there, Alan?"

"I am under the umbrella, Carla."

2.

"The swimmers are leaving. They see the tide coming in."

"Yes, each time the waves break, they wash farther up on shore."

3.

"Bernice and I were looking for shells. We took advantage of the low tide."

"I know. Bernice found a lot of them."

4.

"Alan, are you coming with us to the beach tomorrow?"

"I don't know yet. I will call you."

5.–17. Write each pronoun you identified. On the same line, write *subject* if the pronoun is a subject pronoun. Write *object* if it is an object pronoun.

CUMULATIVE REVIEW

For each sentence, write the pronoun form in parentheses that agrees with its antecedent. Then write *singular* or *plural* next to it.

1. Tom and Orlando are friends, and (he, they) are both interested in oceans.

2. Tom's sister Ruth likes astronomy, so I gave (she, her) a book about the solar system.

3. (Her, She) reads many books on the topic.

4. If Tom and Orlando win the contest, (them, they) will go on a trip.

5. Tom says (him, he) wants to win.

For each sentence, identify the correct plural noun in parentheses.

6. I have three photo (albums, albumes).

7. They are stored in these (boxs, boxes).

8. The photos show my many (friends, friendes).

9. My cousin collects (seashelles, seashells).

10. Do you have any (hobbys, hobbies)?

Write each sentence, changing the underlined word or words to the correct subject or object pronoun or pronouns.

11. Teresa said that <u>her</u> and Lou can go with us.

12. <u>Him and me</u> really like the ocean.

13. <u>Us</u> will have a good time this summer.

14. Can Ned ride with Teresa and <u>I</u>?

POSSESSIVE PRONOUNS

Identify the possessive noun in each sentence.

1. **Franklin turned on his computer.**
2. **Ella typed her report.**
3. **Is your mother a scientist?**
4. **Carmen has a calculator, but its batteries are dead.**
5. **Let's look at the stars with their telescope.**

Write each sentence, using the pronoun form in parentheses that correctly completes the sentence.

6. **Do you know where you left (yours, your) textbook?**
7. **Marie, is this textbook Jud's or (yours, your)?**
8. **Kate and her partner's science folder has more pictures of planets than (our, ours).**
9. **Pat says (mine, my) information is more complete than hers.**
10. **(Theirs, Their) star maps are more detailed than ours.**

POSSESSIVE PRONOUNS

Read the sentences in the notice. Write each possessive pronoun.

DR. K.'s SATELLITE PROGRAM

(1) Join my team. Your future is in space.

(2) My success depends on your gift.

(3) Send your contribution today!

(4) My discoveries can be yours for only $50!

(5) This can be our historic moment.

(6) Ask all your pals to send their $50 right away, too!

(7) Ask Judy to send hers. Ask Jim to send his.

(8) Our future can be theirs!

9.–22. Write each possessive pronoun you identified. On the same line, write *before a noun* if the possessive pronoun is used before a noun. Write *not before a noun* if it is not used before a noun.

CUMULATIVE REVIEW

For each sentence, write the pronoun form in parentheses that fits the sentence best. Write *subject* or *object* to tell what kind of pronoun it is.

1. Theo says that (he, him) likes computers.
2. (Them, They) are planning to present their report to the class.
3. Emma says public speaking isn't easy for (she, her).
4. Theo has already given (she, her) some ideas.
5. Emma and (he, him) enjoy working together.

Identify the conjunction in parentheses that best completes each sentence.

6. Einstein is a good cook, (but, or) Stanley is not.
7. The class is having a special lunch, (but, and) everyone has to bring a dish.
8. Susan can bake a cake, (but, or) she can make custard.
9. Salads are easy for me, (or, and) I always make two.
10. I like carrots, (or, but) I do not like radishes.

Write a possessive pronoun that correctly completes each sentence.

11. Maria asked _____ science teacher if she could join the club.
12. Juan's report is more interesting than _____ .
13. The club is giving _____ first open house in November.
14. Dr. Kronkheit was not asked to deliver _____ report.
15. The students will hang _____ posters on the wall.

CASE

Skill Reminder

- The **case** of a personal pronoun is the form that shows how the pronoun is used in a sentence. A subject pronoun is in the subjective case. An object pronoun is in the objective case. A possessive pronoun is in the possessive case.

Write the pronoun in each sentence. Then identify whether it is *subjective* or *objective*, depending on its case.

1. You must tell Melba about the moon landing.
2. This book will describe the landing for her.
3. I wonder how stepping onto the moon feels.
4. Earth has an atmosphere surrounding it.
5. There are the atmosphere, stratosphere, and ionosphere; beyond them, all is black.
6. The astronauts' photographs teach us about Earth.

Write each sentence, choosing the pronoun form in parentheses that completes the sentence best.

7. Mark, the moon is rising to (yours, your) left.
8. Kate says (her, she) telescope is quite large.
9. Valerie and Lea tried to see the moon's surface through (theirs, their) telescope.
10. Their telescope is larger than (our, ours).
11. Marty focuses (he, his) telescope on a star.

CASE

Each of these sentences is part of an entry in a log describing Earth as seen from space. Write each pronoun, and name the case of the pronoun.

1. The captain said, "We are more than 100 miles above Earth and can see its surface."

2. Mark and Dane said that they were having trouble keeping their bodies upright.

3. The beauty of our blue planet overwhelmed the commander, and she could not say a word.

4. Finally, the commander spoke to the NASA staff and described to them what she saw.

5. Storms and rivers, hurricanes and mountains—the crew could see them clearly.

6. The astronauts sensed that this special view of Earth was theirs alone.

7. One of our crew said, "We can see the beauty, but the pollution and destruction are visible, too."

8. The project chief at NASA said he wanted more pictures of Earth from us.

9.–10. Write two sentences using pronouns. Write which case you have used.

Read the passage, and choose a word that belongs in each space.

Joe's science class was studying about plants. "Seeds move around quite a bit," said Joe. "How do (1) get from one place to another?"

"Well, for one thing, Joe," said (2) teacher, Mr. Griff, "wind carries (3). Can (4) think of another possible way?" Joe shook his head. "Molly is raising her hand. What ways can (5) think of, Molly?" Mr. Griff asked.

1. A them
   B they
   C theirs
   D their

2. F your
   G its
   H yours
   J his

3. A them
   B they
   C it
   D yours

4. F I
   G yours
   H you
   J your

5. A her
   B she
   C you
   D hers

REFLEXIVE PRONOUNS

Identify the reflexive pronoun in each sentence. Write whether the pronoun is *singular* or *plural*, and then write the word to which the pronoun refers.

1. The girl found herself in the kitchen.
2. She baked the cake all by herself.
3. The oven turned itself off automatically.
4. Lena's friends reminded themselves that she was a good cook.
5. I treated myself to a second piece of cake.

Write each sentence, using the correct pronoun from the two in parentheses.

6. I placed (me, myself) near Granddaddy's chair.
7. Granddaddy said that he never forgave (him, himself) for his actions.
8. He wanted Hattie to have the best for (her, herself).
9. He promised (him, himself) that he would find something to put in the box.
10. Did Hattie open the box that Granddaddy had given (her, herself)?

REFLEXIVE PRONOUNS

Without reflexive pronouns, these sentences would sound rather strange. Write each sentence, using a reflexive pronoun that makes sense.

1. After she put up Spencer's birthday banner, the nurse felt pleased with the nurse.

2. "Is Hattie coming by Hattie?" Granddaddy asked me.

3. "Is Granddaddy talking to you or to Granddaddy?" Momma asked.

4. I think Granddaddy Spencer is worrying Granddaddy sick over Hattie.

5. Momma told Granddaddy, "I made the cake all by me."

6. Hattie and Otto enjoyed Hattie and Otto at the party.

7. We told us that we shouldn't eat too much cake.

8. The guests clapped and talked among the guests.

9.–10. Write two sentences of your own. Use reflexive pronouns.

CUMULATIVE REVIEW

Write each sentence. Choose the correct pronoun.

1. Granddaddy smiled at (I, me).

2. I could see that (he, him) was worried.

3. Hattie told Spencer, "(We, Us) haven't seen each other in more than seventy years."

4. I watched (they, them) as they talked together.

Some of the sentences below contain pronoun errors. Write the sentences, correcting the errors. If a sentence contains no errors, write *No mistake.*

5. Is that box yours?

6. I can't find mine cake knife.

7. Mom says that that cake plate is her's.

8. The dessert plates are ours', I think.

9. Did you open you're present?

Write each sentence. Choose the correct pronoun.

10. Hattie sat (her, herself) down next to Spencer.

11. Hattie and Spencer talked (them, themselves) out.

12. I told (me, myself) everything was all right now.

13. Momma hummed to (her, herself) while she cut the cake.

ADJECTIVES AND ARTICLES

- An **adjective** is a word that describes a noun or a pronoun.
- Adjectives can tell *which one, what kind,* or *how many.* Adjectives may come before the nouns they describe. An adjective may also follow a verb such as *is, seems,* or *appears.*
- The adjectives *a, an,* and *the* are called **articles**. The article *the* refers to a person, place, thing, or idea.
- Use *a* before a word that begins with a consonant sound. Use *an* before a word that begins with a vowel sound.

Identify the adjective or adjectives in each sentence. Write whether the adjective tells *which one, what kind,* or *how many.*

1. The kit had been on order for two weeks.
2. It arrived in a brown box.
3. Jason opened it with great anticipation.
4. The gift seemed wonderful.

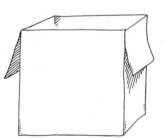

Write the adjective and the word it describes.

5. However, the box was empty.
6. All he wanted was one kit.
7. Jason was sad at the discovery.
8. Someone had made an unfortunate mistake.

Write each sentence, using the correct form of the article in parentheses.

9. The company had sent Jason (a, an) empty box.
10. Jason's mother tried to make (a, an) telephone call.

ADJECTIVES AND ARTICLES

Write each sentence. Identify each adjective, and write the word the adjective describes. Then write whether the adjective tells *which one*, *what kind*, or *how many*.

1. Birthdays are special occasions.
2. Do you like chocolate cake?
3. The decorations seem colorful.
4. Mom bought long streamers and funny hats.
5. Jason invited eight close friends from school.

Write each sentence, replacing each blank with an article that makes sense.

6. Jason wrote _____ company _____ angry letter.
7. He said that his birthday was _____ pretty neat day.
8. When he opened his presents, he saved _____ biggest one for last.
9. Except for _____ lot of Styrofoam, _____ box was empty.
10. _____ boy wanted to learn how _____ tadpole turns into _____ frog.

CUMULATIVE REVIEW

Write the sentences. Choose the correct pronoun.

1. Jason asked (him, himself) how this could have happened.
2. Mom asked Dad if (he, himself) wanted to write the letter.
3. Mom told (her, herself) that no one could make such a mistake.
4. The whole family laughed (them, themselves) silly at the first reply.
5. Grandmother asked Jason if (he, him) would like to go to the zoo.
6. Jason asked whether (they, them) could see the frogs and toads.
7. Grandmother said that seeing the giraffes and tigers would also please (she, her).
8. Jason agreed that (they, them) should see as many animals as possible.

Identify each adjective. Write the word it describes.

9. Tall trees lined the broad walks at the zoo.
10. Jason noticed that the leaves were red, yellow, and rust.
11. A strong breeze blew, and clouds raced across a gray sky.
12. Jason wondered whether colder weather was on the way.
13. Dark clouds were approaching quickly.
14. Large drops of rain began to fall.
15. Did you see that long bolt of lightning?

PROPER ADJECTIVES

Identify the proper adjectives in each of the sentences below. Then write the proper nouns from which they are formed.

1. The monster visited Chicago, an American city.

2. After a few days, the spaceship traveled to London, the British capital.

3. The monster wanted to eat some Indonesian food, however.

4. Next, his taste buds longed for a Parisian restaurant.

5. Later, the monster toured the Italian countryside.

Write each sentence, replacing the words in parentheses with a proper adjective. Underline the adjective you wrote.

6. Lots of cowboy stories take place in a (in the Southwest) setting.

7. Do you like stories about (from Mars) monsters?

8. Are (from America) writers the only ones who write science fiction?

9. Many (from Persia) stories deal with mythical beings.

10. That book has (from Arabia) design patterns.

PROPER ADJECTIVES

Change each of the proper nouns below to a proper adjective. Then use each proper adjective in a sentence of your own.

1. **Russia**

2. **Texas**

3. **Poland**

4. **Canada**

Use a dictionary to find the irregularly formed proper adjectives that are called for below. Then write the sentences, using the correct proper adjectives.

5. **(From Greece) statues are found in many museums.**

6. **Grieg was a (from Norway) composer.**

7. **Have you been to the exhibit of (from Peru) weavings?**

8. **My jeans have more holes than a piece of (from Switzerland) cheese.**

9. **(From France) people are famous for their breads.**

10. **People in Mexico speak (from Spain).**

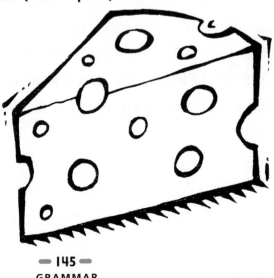

CUMULATIVE REVIEW

Identify the adjective. Then write the word that the adjective describes.

1. William Joyce says that it takes a long time to create a good book.

2. The shortest time he spent on a book was two months.

3. His first drawings may be loose.

4. If Joyce is unhappy with a painting, he starts over from scratch.

Write each sentence. Choose the correct pronoun.

5. Joyce's parents let (him, himself) take art lessons.

6. Joyce promised (him, himself) that he would write a book about monsters.

7. Many artists train (them, themselves) to draw realistically.

8. I enjoyed (me, myself) when I looked through Joyce's scrapbook.

Write each sentence, replacing the proper noun in parentheses with the correct proper adjective.

9. Claude Monet was a (France) artist.

10. Have you seen photographs of the (Brazil) Amazon?

11. Tina would like to visit the (Switzerland) Alps.

12. Curry is an ingredient in many (India) dishes.

COMPARING WITH ADJECTIVES

Identify each adjective that is used to make a comparison. Then write the basic form of the adjective.

1. **"Today is your younger sister's birthday," she said.**

2. **"The nicest present of all would be a mess of jambalaya."**

3. **Mama bought the freshest crabs and shrimp she could find.**

4. **Jambalaya is even spicier than onion soup.**

Write each sentence, using the correct form of the adjective in parentheses.

5. **Saving five dollars was (difficult) than Louis had thought.**

6. **The gospel music was (inspiring) than the sermon.**

7. **Mama's jambalaya was the (delicious) food that Louis had ever tasted.**

Write the correct form of the adjective in parentheses.

8. **Nothing is (bad) than a bad cold.**

9. **Louis felt (well) than he had before he took the medicine.**

10. **The (bad) thing of all would be if the horn had been sold.**

COMPARING WITH ADJECTIVES

Complete each sentence by writing the correct comparing form of one of the adjectives from the box below. Use each adjective only once.

crunchy	fine	bitter
fresh	sweet	great

1. Peaches are ____ than onions.
2. Those greens are probably the ____ I've ever eaten.
3. Carrots are ____ than spinach.
4. The shrimp are ____ than the crabs today.
5. Mama fixed the ____ meal we had ever eaten.
6. No one cooks jambalaya with a ____ variety of vegetables than Mama.

Write each sentence, using the correct form of the adjective in parentheses.

7. Louis Armstrong became one of the (famous) trumpeters in the history of jazz.
8. No musician was (popular) with the public than Louis.
9. Many jazz fans agree that Louis was the (exciting) performer of his century.
10. For many jazz lovers, Satchmo remains the (great) of all jazz musicians.

CUMULATIVE REVIEW

Write the proper adjective formed from the proper noun in parentheses. You may use a dictionary if necessary.

1. Satchmo was very popular with (France) people.
2. (Scandinavia) fans loved to hear him play, too.
3. There is no doubt that jazz is a (Europe) favorite.
4. Wherever Satchmo sang and played, he made friends for (America) music.

Identify the adjective in each sentence below. Write the word that the adjective describes.

5. That album has beautiful photographs.
6. The library keeps many rare recordings in a special room.
7. Librarians handle older records with great care.
8. An album signed by Satchmo is still a valuable item.

Write each sentence, using the correct adjective form.

9. People could buy Satchmo's records because they were (cheaper, more cheap) than ever before.
10. One of Louis Armstrong's (famousest, most famous) recordings is "Hello, Dolly."
11. Was that song (more popular, popularer) than his "Mack the Knife"?

MAIN AND HELPING VERBS

- A **verb** is a word or group of words that expresses action or being. When a verb includes two or more words, it is called a **verb phrase**. The **main verb** is the most important word in a verb phrase.

- A **helping verb** can work with the main verb to tell about an action. These words are often used as helping verbs:

am	was	has	does	could
is	were	have	do	would
are	will	had	did	should

- Sometimes other words, such as *not*, appear between a helping verb and a main verb.

Identify the verb phrase in each sentence. Then write the main verb.

1. **Phyllis Cyr had taught Evelyn the beauty of ballet.**

2. **Evelyn was working hard in class.**

3. **She could perform turns and jumps gracefully.**

4. **With hard work, she would master jazz, tap, and other styles.**

Identify each main verb and helping verb.

5. **Evelyn was earning extra money through giving lessons for younger students.**

6. **Mrs. Cisneros had taken a job at the front desk of the studio.**

7. **By the age of fourteen, Evelyn was facing a decision.**

8. **She could never stop her ballet lessons.**

MAIN AND HELPING VERBS

Write each sentence, adding the word in parentheses to the verb phrase.

1. Evelyn would miss her sports activities. (always)

2. She must stop ballet lessons. (never)

Write each sentence, adding either a helping verb or a main verb to complete the verb phrase. Choose from the list below. You may use a word more than once.

had	could	was	would
might	growing	placed	

3. Every day after school, Evelyn _____ head straight to the ballet studio.

4. She stayed late so she _____ practice longer.

5. She knew that someday she _____ learn roles from famous ballets.

6. Evelyn was _____ more and more confident about her ability.

7. To her surprise, she _____ awarded summer scholarships at two different schools.

8. When ballet school started in New York, Evelyn was _____ in a very slow class.

9. By the end of summer, she _____ become discouraged.

CUMULATIVE REVIEW

Read the passage below and choose the word or group of words that belongs in each space.

   Many famous ballets were written by the (1) composer Peter Ilyich Tchaikovsky. Two of them are *Sleeping Beauty* and *Swan Lake*. The leading role in *Sleeping Beauty* is one of the (2) roles to dance. Evelyn Cisneros promised (3) that one day she (4) the role. After her performance, the audience showed (5) approval with a standing ovation.

1. A Russish
   B Russian
   C Russia
   D Russ

2. F more difficult
   G difficulter
   H difficultest
   J most difficult

3. A she
   B her
   C herself
   D herselves

4. F will perform
   G would perform
   H had performed
   J was performing

5. A their
   B themselves
   C them
   D they's

ACTION AND LINKING VERBS

- An **action verb** tells what the subject of a sentence does, did, or will do.
- An action verb is often followed by a **direct object**, which receives the action of the verb.
- A **linking verb** connects the subject of a sentence to a noun, a pronoun, or an adjective in the predicate that renames or describes the subject. The most common linking verbs are forms of *be* and forms of other words such as *appear, become, feel, grow, look, seem,* and *taste.*

Identify the action verb or the linking verb. Then write the direct object if there is one.

1. They bought some bread at a convenience store.
2. The bread was a gift.
3. As they drove up the street, the tires of the car scattered the fall leaves.
4. The cat in the street was orange.
5. Miata was nervous about her visit with the woman.
6. She walked up the steps, knocked at the screen door, and peered inside.

Write each sentence. Draw a line under each linking verb. Circle the word in the predicate that renames or describes the subject. Write *noun, pronoun,* or *adjective* to describe the word.

7. Doña Carmen's walk seemed a shuffle.
8. Her face appeared soft, and her hair was gray.
9. Doña Carmen's husband was her opponent.

ACTION AND LINKING VERBS

Write each sentence. Draw one line under each action verb and two lines under each linking verb. In sentences with linking verbs, circle the word in the predicate that renames or describes the subject. Write *noun, pronoun,* or *adjective* to describe the word. In sentences with action verbs, circle the direct object if there is one.

1. The old woman's eyes sparkled when she recalled her husband.

2. Her voice grew stronger.

3. Her husband disapproved of the smart young women.

4. For Doña Carmen, the children of the town were the future.

5. She won the election for mayor three times.

Write each sentence, completing it with a verb from the box. Then write whether the verb is an *action* or a *linking* verb.

became	ran	appeared	chose

6. In the election for mayor, Doña Carmen _____ against her husband.

7. The people of Aguascalientes _____ Doña Carmen as their leader.

8. Many young women in the town _____ students at the university.

9. Doña Carmen _____ happy with Miata's plans for her school.

CUMULATIVE REVIEW

Write the correct adjective form.

1. Mom made the (best, bestest) breakfast that Miata had ever eaten.

2. To Joey, tortillas tasted (better, more good) than eggs.

3. Is Carlos Santana (famouser, more famous) than Eddie Olmos?

4. Miata's mother told her to be home by two o'clock at the (later, latest).

Write the sentences below. Underline the verbs or verb phrases. Then identify the main verb and the helping verb.

5. By the middle of November, most of the leaves had fallen from the trees.

6. On our trip downtown, we saw a few geraniums in pots on the steps of houses.

7. Next spring, the azaleas and jasmine will bloom again.

8. Many people will work in their gardens and will enjoy the flowers and plants.

Write each sentence. Draw one line under each action verb and two lines under each linking verb.

9. Was Rudy a very serious candidate?

10. He promised the students ice cream and more recess.

11. For Miata, the election was more important.

12. If she won the election, Miata would be a good leader.

PRESENT TENSE

- The **tense of a verb** tells you the time of action. A **present-tense verb** shows that the action is happening now or that it happens over and over.

- When the subject is singular and it is not *I* or *you*, add *-s* to most verbs to show the present tense. Add *-es* to verbs ending in *s, ch, x,* or *z*. If the verb ends in a consonant plus *y*, change the *y* to *i* and add *-es*.

Identify all the present-tense verbs in the sentences.

1. Perhaps a tree is better than a person.
2. As the children form a line, Jean hears Shirley's laugh.
3. Jean counts her steps every day and joins the right line.
4. After the children return to their desks, Miss Marr announces a mental arithmetic test.
5. Jean grasps her special fat pencil.

Write each sentence. Choose the verb form in parentheses that agrees with the subject.

6. All the students (marks, mark) their own papers.
7. Ruth Dayton (passes, pass) behind Jean's desk.
8. Miss Marr (give, gives) the answers to the questions.
9. Jean (put, puts) ten neat check marks on her paper.
10. Then Ruth and Stella (march, marches) up to Jean's desk.

PRESENT TENSE

Write each sentence. If the subject and the verb are plural, make them singular. If the subject and the verb are singular, make them plural.

1. The students take an arithmetic test.
2. The geography lesson is interesting.
3. We like the new teacher.
4. The children write a story.
5. The boy draws imaginative pictures.
6. Do the girls know the truth?
7. The pencils on this table need to be sharpened.
8. The visitor enjoys the class.

Write each sentence, using the present-tense form of the verb in parentheses.

9. Meredith and Sam (love) apple pie.
10. Where (is) the eggs?
11. Sam (help) with the dough.
12. It (taste) delicious!

CUMULATIVE REVIEW

Write each sentence. Underline the verb or verb phrase. Then write the main verb.

1. Jean Little is learning about snakes in her science class.
2. Have you ever seen a python?
3. If not, the size of this snake could surprise you.
4. Some of these snakes are more than 18 feet long.

Write each sentence. Draw one line under each action verb and two lines under each linking verb. Circle the direct object if there is one.

5. Some pythons live in dense forests.
6. They eat small mammals.
7. They appear dangerous, but they are harmless to humans.
8. Sometimes they go for long periods without food.

Write each sentence. Choose the verb form in parentheses that agrees with the subject.

9. A female python (lay, lays) anywhere from eight to one hundred eggs.
10. The eggs (hatch, hatches) about two months later.
11. The young snakes (grow, grows) fairly rapidly.
12. By the age of five, they (reach, reaches) a length of 11 feet!

PAST AND FUTURE TENSES

- A verb in the **past tense** shows that the action happened in the past. Form the past tense of most verbs by adding *ed*. If the verb ends in *e*, add *d*. If the verb ends in a consonant plus *y*, change the *y* to *i* and add *ed*.

- A verb in the **future tense** shows that the action will happen in the future. To form the future tense of a verb, use the helping verb *will* with the main verb.

Write the verb or verb phrase for each sentence. Then identify the tense of the verb as *past* or *future*.

1. Leigh's diary started on Thursday, March 1.
2. On that day, he carried a new lunch box to school.
3. His classmates will be curious when they see it.
4. Someone at school lifted the salami and cheese rolls.
5. Maybe the thief will confess.

Write each sentence, using the correct tense of the verb in parentheses.

6. Yesterday, Leigh (experiment) with some new rhymes.
7. Tomorrow, he (visit) Barry's house after school.
8. Earlier, Barry (mention) that he wanted a burglar alarm for his room.
9. Barry hopes that Leigh (help) him make a burglar alarm.
10. A few minutes ago, Barry's sisters (arrive).

PAST AND FUTURE TENSES

Write each sentence, changing the tense of the verb to the tense in parentheses.

1. Mom packs Leigh's lunch carefully. (past)
2. Leigh places his lunch box behind the partition. (past)
3. The alarm bell worked. (future)
4. Leigh worries. (past)
5. He carries the lunch box to the cafeteria. (future)

Write each sentence. Change past-tense verbs to future tense and future-tense verbs to past tense.

6. The alarm inside the lunch box created a terrible racket.
7. The noise carried throughout the house.
8. Mom will rush to Leigh's door.
9. Leigh will demonstrate the alarm for her.
10. The sandwich will muffle the bell.

Draw the chart. Fill in the verb forms that are missing.

PRESENT	PAST	FUTURE
11. plant		
12. cook		will cook
13. dance	danced	
14. open		
15. walk		

CUMULATIVE REVIEW

Identify the verb or verb phrase in each sentence. Then write *present,* *past,* or *future* to identify the tense of the verb.

1. Yesterday Miss Neely, the librarian, asked Leigh a question.
2. "Will you finish your story for the Young Writer's Yearbook?"
3. Someday Leigh will meet a famous author.
4. He decides on a story topic.

Write each sentence, choosing the correct verb form.

5. Leigh and his father (drive, drives) through Pacheco Pass.
6. The truck (reach, reaches) a sharp curve.
7. Dad (handle, handles) the rig skillfully.
8. The smell of grapes (fill, fills) the air.

Identify the verb in each sentence. Write whether it is an action verb or a linking verb.

9. The road signs seem blurry.
10. Those sharp curves frighten me.
11. Dad shifted to a lower gear.
12. He is a good driver.
13. Leigh saw a high peak.
14. The leaves were yellow.

PRINCIPAL PARTS OF VERBS

- The four basic forms of a verb are its **principal parts**. These forms are the *infinitive*, the *present participle*, the *past*, and the *past participle*. Participles in verb phrases are forms used with helping verbs.

Infinitive	Present Participle	Past	Past Participle
(to) play	(is) playing	played	(have, has, had) played
(to) move	(is) moving	moved	(have, has, had) moved

Write whether the underlined verb form(s) in each sentence are *present participles, past-tense verbs,* or *past participles.*

1. The sun was <u>shining</u> brightly.
2. The girls were <u>talking</u> and <u>shouting</u>.
3. Maddie <u>listened</u> to the happy sounds.
4. Wanda timidly <u>approached</u> the group of girls.
5. She has never <u>talked</u> to them.
6. Wanda had <u>touched</u> Peggy's arm.

Write each sentence with the correct form of the verb in parentheses.

7. Wanda is (speak) to Peggy.
8. She has (repeat) her words.
9. Maddie remembers how Peggy (ridicule) Wanda that day.
10. The day no longer (seem) beautiful.
11. Peggy has (ask) Wanda about the hundred dresses every day.
12. Maddie is (think) about Wanda.

PRINCIPAL PARTS OF VERBS

Write the present and past participles of each verb listed. Remember that some verbs change their spelling when *-ing* or *-ed* is added.

1. **wrap**
2. **picture**
3. **admire**
4. **decide**
5. **hurry**

Write each sentence, using the correct form of the verb in parentheses.

6. **Are one hundred dresses (hang) in the closet?**
7. **Peggy is (hope) to win the drawing contest.**
8. **The teacher has (announce) the winners.**
9. **Everyone has (stop) to look at the drawings.**
10. **Had Wanda (believe) she would win?**

11.–15. Write whether each verb form written in items 6.–10. is a *present participle*, a *past-tense verb*, or a *past participle*.

CUMULATIVE REVIEW

Identify the verb or verbs in each sentence. Then write whether they are *present, past,* or *future* tense.

1. Maddie often wears Peggy's old dresses.
2. Peggy teases Wanda.
3. Will Maddie tell Peggy what she thinks?
4. Maddie wrote Peggy a note.

5.–8. Here is the beginning of a note from Maddie to Peggy. Identify each helping verb and each main verb.

	Dear Peggy,
	I do not think you should tease Wanda
	anymore. I can imagine how Wanda is
	feeling.

Label the underlined verb form in each sentence as *present participle, past,* or *past participle.*

9. The art teacher <u>encouraged</u> her students.
10. Have you <u>finished</u> your painting?
11. My sister is <u>creating</u> a collage.
12. I wish I had <u>entered</u> the contest.

Write each sentence, using the verb form or tense found in parentheses.

13. Maddie sharpens her pencil. (present participle)
14. The scene flashes before her eyes. (past)

REGULAR AND IRREGULAR VERBS

- **Regular verbs** are verbs that end with *ed* in the past tense.

- **Irregular verbs** are verbs that do not end with *ed* in the past tense. They have special spellings for the past tense and the past participle.

- The irregular verbs *be* and *have* also have special spellings for the present tense.

- This chart shows some irregular verbs:

INFINITIVE	PAST	PAST PARTICIPLE
(to) bring	brought	(have, has, had) brought
(to) do	did	(have, has, had) done
(to) know	knew	(have, has, had) known
(to) say	said	(have, has, had) said
(to) speak	spoke	(have, has, had) spoken
(to) think	thought	(have, has, had) thought

Identify the verb in each sentence. Write whether it is *regular* or *irregular*.

1. Nick and Janet walked home after school.

2. They said little to each other.

3. Nick spoke to Janet about something.

Write the correct verb form for each sentence.

4. "Have you (doed, done) your exercises?" Mrs. Granger asked.

5. Nick had (bringed, brought) his homework to class.

6. Sarah (knew, knowed) that there was a mistake in the first sentence.

REGULAR AND IRREGULAR VERBS

Write the past tense and past participle of each verb.

1. **buy**
2. **do**
3. **know**

Identify each verb or verb phrase. Write whether the *present participle, past,* or *past participle* form is used.

4. **The Penny Pantry stocked pens.**
5. **The next day, Nick had come into the store.**
6. **"A frindle, please," he had said to the lady behind the counter.**
7. **By the look on her face, she had not understood the word.**
8. **Six days later, Janet was standing at the same counter.**

Write each sentence, using the correct form of the verb in parentheses.

9. **Yesterday, Nick and Janet (walk) home after school.**
10. **Janet told Nick she had (see) something in the street.**
11. **Nick (think) about the class.**
12. **What had Mrs. Granger (say) about words and meanings?**
13. **By the following afternoon, Nick's plan was (take) shape.**
14. **Nick is (get) nervous.**

Read the passage and choose the word or group of words that belongs in each space.

Last week, Mrs. Granger (1) to the class about words. "Some words (2) quite like their meaning," she (3). "For example, the word *buzz* (4) you think of the sound of a bee." By the time class ended, Nick (5) of several more examples, including *spatter* and *murmur*.

1. **A** speaks
   B has spoke
   C spoke
   D speaked

2. **A** sound
   B sounds
   C sounding
   D had sounded

3. **A** saying
   B say
   C sayed
   D said

4. **A** makes
   B was making
   C maked
   D had made

5. **A** thinks
   B had thought
   C think
   D are thought

PERFECT TENSES

- There are three perfect tenses—**present perfect, past perfect, and future perfect**. The perfect tenses are made up of the past participle and a form of the helping verb *have*. The form of the helping verb shows the tense.

- A verb in the present-perfect tense shows that the action started to happen sometime in the past. The action may have just happened or may still be happening.

- A verb in the past-perfect tense shows that the action happened before a specific time in the past.

- A verb in the future-perfect tense shows that the action will be completed before a specific time in the future.

Identify the verb phrase in each sentence. Then write whether the tense is *present perfect, past perfect,* or *future perfect.*

1. By sailing time, we had found a corner out of the damp and cold.

2. My mother and brother have been seasick several times.

3. According to one sailor, by evening a storm will have gathered.

4. Birds with black wings have circled the ship.

5. Before the big storm, the sailors had raced to furl the sails.

Write the sentence with the verb and tense shown in parentheses.

6. "Quick! A man (*fall*, present perfect) overboard!"

7. If the sailors don't hurry, he (*drown*, future perfect) before help comes.

8. By the time I looked, the man (*catch*, past perfect) hold of a rope.

PERFECT TENSES

Write each sentence, changing the verb to the form indicated in parentheses.

1. Someone thought of the iron pick. (present perfect)
2. The sailors place a new post underneath the beam. (present perfect)
3. By nightfall, they patch all the leaks. (future perfect)
4. Our ship sails on safely. (present perfect)
5. Six weeks later, we still do not see land. (past perfect)

Write each sentence. Change verbs in the present tense to present perfect and verbs in the past tense to past perfect.

6. We desire freedom in a new land.
7. We embarked on a long journey.
8. We saw signs of land.
9. We arrive in America.
10. We find a place to live.

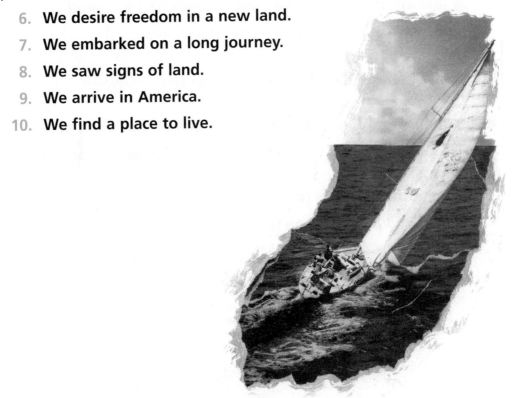

CUMULATIVE REVIEW

Identify each underlined verb as *regular* or *irregular*.

1. When the storm <u>began</u>, the wind <u>howled</u>.
2. The seas <u>became</u> as high as mountains.
3. Fear <u>took</u> hold of many of the passengers.
4. They <u>expected</u> the worst.

Identify the underlined form of the main verb in each sentence as present participle, past, or past participle.

5. After the storm, we <u>dried</u> our clothes.
6. After a few hours, my shoes <u>felt</u> dry at last.
7. By late afternoon, however, more clouds had <u>gathered</u>.
8. "Another storm is <u>coming</u>," I told my father.

Write each sentence, using the verb and the tense shown in parentheses.

9. For hours now, I (*stand*, present perfect) on the ship's deck.
10. The sailors (*climb*, past perfect) up to the rigging to hoist the sails.
11. "By nightfall, a storm (*break*, future perfect)," one sailor said.
12. "Look how rough the sea (*grow*, present perfect)!"

CONTRACTIONS AND NEGATIVES

- A **contraction** is the shortened form of two words. An **apostrophe** takes the place of one or more letters that are left out.
- A word that has "no" or "not" in its meaning is called a **negative**. The words *never, no, nobody, none, not, nothing,* and *nowhere* are common negatives. Use only one negative in a sentence.
- Do not confuse a possessive pronoun, such as *its* or *their,* with a contraction, such as *it's* or *they're.*

Write each sentence. Underline the negatives. Then circle any contractions.

1. In Ben Franklin's day, families were never without an almanac.
2. These books were not expensive.
3. Nowhere could you find better information or more useful advice.
4. It's also true that the almanacs contained jokes.
5. We're still familiar today with many of these one-liners.

Write each sentence, using the correct contraction for the underlined words.

6. I have learned a lot about the life of Ben Franklin.
7. He is one of the most interesting people in American history.
8. Would not Franklin's life make a good movie?
9. Was he not twenty-six when he thought of his first big idea?
10. As you will see, *Poor Richard's Almanack* was a best-seller.

CONTRACTIONS AND NEGATIVES

Write the correct contraction for each pair of words.

1. **you are**
2. **I have**
3. **he is**
4. **could not**
5. **are not**
6. **they will**
7. **she had**
8. **they are**
9. **will not**
10. **has not**

Write each sentence, using the correct word or words in parentheses.

11. **Ben Franklin hadn't (ever, never) been to London.**
12. **The people of Pennsylvania couldn't think of (anybody, nobody) better to send there.**
13. **Once he got to London, Franklin didn't spare (any, no) expense.**
14. **No one (dressed, didn't dress) in finer clothes than he did.**
15. **Mrs. Stevenson never served Franklin (nothing, anything) but his favorite foods.**

CUMULATIVE REVIEW

Identify the verb or verb phrase in each sentence. Write whether it is *regular* or *irregular*.

1. Ben Franklin lived like a king in London.
2. He ordered new spectacles.
3. Mrs. Stevenson's cat never sat in Franklin's favorite chair.
4. Over the years, England had become more stubborn.

Identify the tense of each underlined verb as present perfect, past perfect, or future perfect.

5. A Scottish visitor <u>has come</u> to see Franklin in Paris.
6. "Sir, you <u>have left</u> some state papers on your desk in full view!" he told Franklin.
7. "Do not worry. By nightfall I <u>will have cleaned</u> up everything," Franklin assured him.
8. The important thing was that Franklin <u>had accomplished</u> his goals.

Write each sentence, using the correct word in parentheses.

9. The French ladies hadn't (ever, never) seen anyone more charming than Franklin.
10. (Their, They're) happy he has come to Paris.
11. (Its, It's) a delightful city.
12. Franklin couldn't (always, never) be bothered with rules for good behavior.

ADVERBS

- An **adverb** is a word that describes a verb, an adjective, or another adverb.

- An adverb tells *how, when, where,* or *to what extent.* Many adverbs that tell *how* end in *ly.*

- Be careful when you use *good* and *well. Good* is an adjective. *Well* is an adverb, unless it means "healthy."

Underline each adverb. Circle the word it describes. Write whether each adverb tells *how, when, where,* or *to what extent.*

1. The sun shines brightly in the Midwest.

2. Settlers built their homes there with thick walls.

3. The houses were quite cool in summer.

4. Pioneer women quickly learned useful things from the Native Americans.

Write each sentence, replacing the word or words in parentheses with an adverb from the box that gives the correct information.

nearby	very	later	sometimes

5. Black pioneer families (when) felt lonely.

6. The first pioneers made things easier for those who came (when).

7. These families worked (to what extent) hard.

8. Families who lived (where) became neighborly.

ADVERBS

Write each sentence. Underline each adverb. Write the word it describes, and write whether that word is a *verb,* an *adjective,* or another *adverb.*

1. Benjamin Singleton was particularly fond of Bible stories.
2. Singleton and his friends gradually bought land in Kansas.
3. They advertised very widely and attracted new settlers.
4. Soon eight hundred homesteaders arrived in Kansas.
5. People usually called these homesteaders "Exodusters."

Write each sentence, replacing the word or words in parentheses with the correct answer from the box.

joyfully	much	eventually	farther	most

6. Black farmers in Nicodemus (when) prospered.
7. Their numbers grew (to what extent) larger.
8. Some Kansas families moved (where) and built new towns in Nebraska and Oklahoma.
9. Of all the black pioneer communities, Nicodemus and Dunlap remained the (to what extent) famous.
10. Each year, they (how) celebrated Emancipation Day.

CUMULATIVE REVIEW

Write each sentence, using the verb and tense shown in parentheses.

1. By 1907, the Kansas town of Nicodemus (*form*, past perfect) one of the nation's first black baseball teams.

2. Historians (*discover*, present perfect) that the great pitcher Satchel Paige once played in Nicodemus.

3. Before too long, volunteers (*restore*, future perfect) many of the town's buildings.

4. This town (*become*, present perfect) a proud symbol of the legacy of black homesteaders.

Write the correct contraction.

5. could not

6. she had

7. will not

8. they will

9. you are

10. I have

Complete each sentence by replacing the word or words in parentheses with the correct word from the box.

there	quite	gratefully

11. Benjamin Singleton was (to what extent) sure he could lead the families to Kansas.

12. Singleton and his friends bought land (where).

13. Homesteaders (how) accepted the help of their neighbors.

COMPARING WITH ADVERBS

- Adverbs can be used to **compare** actions. When you compare one action with one other action, add *er* to most short adverbs. In most cases, use *more* if the adverb has two or more syllables.

- When you compare one action with two or more other actions, add *est* to most short adverbs. Use *most* if the adverb has two or more syllables.

- The adverbs *much, well,* and *badly* have special forms for comparison: *much, more, most; well, better, best; badly, worse, worst.*

Write the two comparing forms of each adverb.

1. **near**
2. **soon**
3. **freely**
4. **slowly**
5. **well**
6. **regularly**

Write each sentence, using the correct adverb form of the two in parentheses.

7. **Of all his skills, a young cowboy practiced roping (more attentively, most attentively).**

8. **No one on the ranch rode (more proudly, most proudly) than a skilled vaquero.**

9. **Cattle roamed the Texas plains (more widely, most widely) than other animals did.**

COMPARING WITH ADVERBS

Write each sentence, using the correct form of the adverb in parentheses.

1. By the late 1860s, no one was looking (hard) for jobs than discharged Civil War soldiers were.

2. The job that appealed (much) of all to many young men was that of cowhand.

3. This was odd, because cowhands (hardly) saw their families for months at a time.

4. Every day, cowboys worked (long) hours than most workers do now.

5. No one faced danger (bravely) than cowboys did.

Write the two comparing forms for each adverb.

6. eagerly

7. badly

8. responsibly

9. fast

10. late

CUMULATIVE REVIEW

Write each sentence. Underline the negatives. Circle the contractions.

1. Teddy Blue Abbott never saw a cowboy with two six-shooters.
2. Most cowboys weren't sharpshooters.
3. Abbott recalled that he'd work ten to fourteen hours a day.
4. No one was as good as a cowboy at finding a lost calf.

Identify each adverb. Write the word it describes. Then write whether the word it describes is a verb, an adjective, or another adverb.

5. Cowboys often sang to the cattle during drives.
6. Some of these songs became extremely popular.
7. Cowboys rose very early each morning.
8. Youngsters in their teens commonly worked as horse wranglers.

Write each sentence, using the correct comparing form of the adverb in parentheses.

9. No one worked (hard) to earn his pay than a cowboy did.
10. The cowboys dressed (well) of all when they posed for souvenir pictures.
11. Cowboys carried guns (seldom) than you might think from the movies.
12. They rose (early) and went to bed (late) than the other ranch hands did.

PREPOSITIONAL PHRASES

Write each sentence. Underline each prepositional phrase. Identify the preposition and the object of the preposition.

1. Maria Mitchell lived in the nineteenth century.
2. At that time, a woman astronomer was unusual.
3. Mitchell did research on sunspots.
4. She was ahead of her time.
5. In 1847, she discovered a new comet.

Write these sentences, replacing each blank with a preposition that fits the sentence.

6. Dolley Madison was the wife ____ our fourth President.
7. She loved entertaining ____ the White House.
8. She served ice cream ____ her guests.
9. Dolley Madison's finest hour came ____ the War of 1812.
10. She managed to save many ____ her husband's papers, as well as a portrait ____ George Washington.

PREPOSITIONAL PHRASES

Write each sentence. Underline the prepositional phrase in each one. Identify the preposition and its object.

1. Sacajawea did not move west with the explorers.
2. She was captured by Indian enemies and was sold to a French-Canadian trader.
3. She was the main guide for Lewis and Clark's expedition.
4. A river, a mountain peak, and a mountain pass have been named after her.
5. Lewis and Clark would not have been successful without Sacajawea.

Write each sentence. Expand each sentence by adding a prepositional phrase of your own choice.

6. This book is interesting.
7. Our class went on a field trip.
8. I had a good time.
9. The flowers look beautiful.
10. What time will we go?

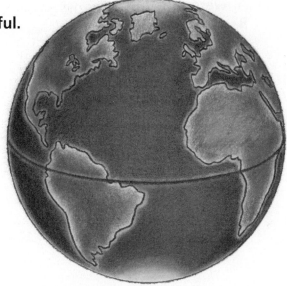

CUMULATIVE REVIEW

Read the passage below and choose the word or group of words that belongs in each space.

    Ellen asked if I wanted to ride (1) the TV studio with her or if I planned to go by myself. We (2) about the new quiz show, "Name This American." A young woman (3) as the Statue of Liberty. Uncle Sam wore a costume of red, white, and blue. A number of distinguished Americans were questioned by members of the panel. You (4) believe it, but the guest I listened to (5) was the inventor of the safety pin.

1. A under
   B from
   C to
   D into

2. F was
   G excited
   H exciting
   J were excited

3. A were dressing
   B was dressed
   C dressing
   D will have dressed

4. F willn't
   G wasn't
   H won't
   J won't not

5. A most attentively
   B mostest attentively
   C more attentively
   D attentiveliest

Additional Practice

ADDITIONAL PRACTICE
Sentences

A. Write whether each word group is a *sentence* or *not a sentence.*

Example:

At the top of the map.
not a sentence

1. Gena looked at the map.
2. Not find New Mexico.
3. She pointed to Arizona.
4. José went to the map.
5. The nearest state.
6. Lies north of the equator.
7. Everyone learned the names of the mountain chains.
8. The longest river in the United States.
9. The states along the coast of the Gulf of Mexico.
10. Gena confused Kansas and Nebraska.
11. Both states quite large.
12. She points to them.
13. The difference between coastal states and inland states.

B. If a group of words is a sentence, write it correctly. Capitalize the first word, and end the sentence with a period. If the group is not a sentence, write *not a sentence*.

Example:

the capital of Illinois is Springfield
The capital of Illinois is Springfield.

14. we memorized the capitals of all the states

15. everyone knew the capital of Arkansas

16. the capital is not always the largest city in the state

17. you should picture the map in your mind

18. the left side is the west side

19. right through the middle of the country

20. that river empties into the Gulf of Mexico

21. the Hudson River valley

22. three people found Delaware right away

23. a map of the thirteen original colonies

Writing Application Write a list of five facts about your state. Use a complete sentence for each fact.

ADDITIONAL PRACTICE

Declarative, Interrogative, Exclamatory, and Imperative Sentences

A. Read each sentence. Tell whether it is *declarative, interrogative, exclamatory,* or *imperative.*

Example:

What is the size of the floor?
interrogative

1. How much paint will we need?
2. Everyone will help on Saturday.
3. Can your brother paint?
4. The barn is quite large.
5. What kind of red paint is that?
6. What a bright color that is!
7. Give that brush to me.
8. Will we finish by sundown?
9. Look at your watch.
10. What a lot of fun that was!

Writing Application Everyone has jobs or chores. Choose one job or chore that you do. Write a paragraph about why that job must be done. Vary your sentences by using statements, questions, exclamations and commands.

B. Write each sentence. Begin and end each sentence correctly.

11. what kind of vegetables will grow here

12. how many rows of tomato plants do you want

13. you will need string

14. spade the ground first

15. we should pull those weeds

16. weeds keep sunlight away from the vegetables

17. what are those dandelions doing here

18. water these little plants carefully

19. bring that large watering can over here

20. these plants need lots of moisture

21. look for my hoe

22. put the garden tools in the garage

23. what a lot of work a garden is

24. do you enjoy working with plants

25. homegrown vegetables taste so wonderful

ADDITIONAL PRACTICE

Subjects and Predicates

A. Read each sentence. Write whether the underlined part is the subject or predicate of the sentence.

Example:

The automobiles ahead of us <u>were not moving</u>.
predicate

1. <u>The highway</u> was covered with water.
2. Martina <u>slowed down quickly</u>.
3. <u>She</u> looked at the cars ahead of us.
4. <u>Two of the cars</u> had water up to the door windows.
5. Martina <u>signaled to the cars behind us</u>.
6. Every car <u>backed up</u>.
7. <u>All of the drivers</u> turned their cars around.
8. Martina <u>followed them to Highway 17</u>.
9. <u>The cars all</u> took the alternate route to high ground.
10. We <u>arrived two hours late but safe and sound</u>.

B. Write each sentence. Then draw a vertical line between the subject and the predicate.

Example:

The heavy rains lasted for three days and nights.
The heavy rains | lasted for three days and nights.

11. The marshy ground was soaked with water.

12. The garbage truck was due in about thirty minutes.

13. Elvis needed to walk to the garbage cans in the back.

14. He pulled on his long rubber boots and his poncho.

15. The garbage bags were heavy.

16. He looked funny sloshing through the soggy grass.

17. One of the garbage bags broke.

18. Aunt Susan laughed out loud at the sight.

19. Elvis almost fell twice.

20. The garbage was placed in the cans despite the driving rain and spongy soil.

21. The pickup truck didn't arrive on time.

22. The two men on the truck complained about the wet roads.

23. We were glad to be inside.

24. Father grumbled about the amount of rain.

25. The birds found plenty of worms for their supper that night.

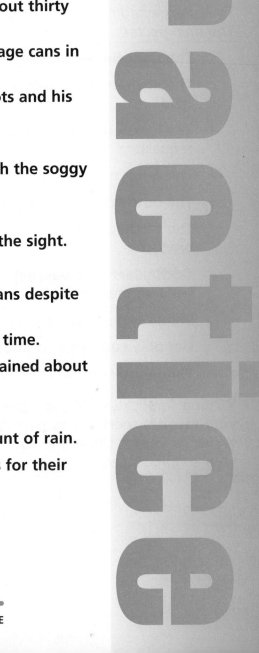

ADDITIONAL PRACTICE

Complete Subjects and Simple Subjects

A. Write each sentence. Underline the complete subject. Then write the simple subject.

Example:

The unexpected news surprised Vanna.
The unexpected news surprised Vanna.   news

1. The right fielder on Vanna's team was sick.

2. The anxious coach asked her to substitute in right field.

3. The inexperienced player was pleased by the coach's request.

4. The other members of the team encouraged her.

5. The outfielder's mitt seemed almost too large.

6. The catcher on Vanna's team gave her some catching practice.

7. Outfielders on a baseball team often must catch fly balls on the run.

8. Vanna's speed as a runner was excellent.

9. Her only concern was about catching every ball.

10. Vanna took her place on the field.

Writing Application Write a persuasive paragraph about your favorite sport. Try to persuade your readers to play or watch the sport. Underline your complete subjects, and circle your simple subjects.

B. Write each sentence. Draw a vertical line after the complete subject. Then underline the simple subject.

Example:

The young girl enjoyed playing on the baseball team.
The young <u>girl</u> | enjoyed playing on the baseball team.

11. **The very first batter struck out.**

12. **The pitcher on the mound concentrated on each pitch.**

13. **The first baseman caught a ground ball.**

14. **Vanna's team was ahead by two runs before the end of the third inning.**

15. **The ninth inning brought a crisis.**

16. **The other team almost tied the game.**

17. **The opposing team's pitcher got on base with a single to center field.**

18. **Their best hitter came to bat next.**

19. **She hit a fly ball into right field.**

20. **Vanna's last-minute catch produced wild cheers from her teammates.**

ADDITIONAL PRACTICE

Complete Predicates and Simple Predicates

A. Read each sentence. The complete predicate of the sentence is underlined. Write the simple predicate.

Example:

The young girl saw jewels of every color and size.
saw

1. Violetta looked in amazement at the beautiful light-blue stones.
2. The smiling clerk told Violetta about them.
3. The stones on the counter were called *turquoise*.
4. Violetta could not believe the careful workmanship.
5. No stone seemed the same as any other.
6. Each of the pieces was of a slightly different shape.
7. She saw other stones, such as lapis lazuli and amethyst.
8. The turquoise rings were her favorites.
9. The young girl made a decision right away.
10. She would learn the art of jewelry making.

Writing Application Write several sentences about a craft or an art you know or would like to learn. Underline your complete predicates, and circle your simple predicates.

B. Write each sentence. Draw a vertical line between the complete subject and the complete predicate. Then underline the simple predicate.

Example:

The Martins enjoyed the annual crafts fair.
The Martins | <u>enjoyed</u> the annual crafts fair.

11. The crafts exhibit contained many booths.

12. One of them was devoted to jewelry.

13. Rings, pendants, and bracelets glistened on a rack.

14. One of the most challenging tasks in jewelry making is the creation of the setting for the stone in a ring.

15. Some of the most unusual settings held pieces of amethyst or onyx.

16. The colors of the stones were quite varied.

17. A tiger-eye ring was especially beautiful.

18. All of the jewelry had been made by local craft workers.

19. Jewelry was a hobby for many of them.

20. Their work was comparable to that of a professional jeweler.

ADDITIONAL PRACTICE

Compound Subjects and Compound Predicates

A. Read each sentence. Write the compound subject. Underline the word that joins the simple subjects.

Example:

The puppy and the kitten get along well with each other.
The puppy <u>and</u> the kitten

1. The veterinarian and her assistant examined the two animals.

2. Bud and Marissa smiled proudly.

3. A kitten or a puppy can be a special joy for a family.

4. Kittens and puppies usually are very curious.

5. Mr. Gundersen and his wife had bought their children a puppy.

6. A cat and one kitten found their way to the Gundersens' house.

7. Mrs. Gundersen or Marissa fed the animals on the back porch.

8. The kitten and its mother slept there every night.

9. Ads and phone calls produced no owner for the animals.

10. The cat, the puppy, and the kitten were soon the best of friends.

Writing Applications What are some of the responsibilities of pet ownership? Brainstorm with a partner, and then write a short essay on the topic. Use some compound subjects and compound predicates.

B. Read each sentence. Write the compound predicate, and underline the word that joins the simple predicates.

Example:

Tourists carry maps or ask questions.
carry maps <u>or</u> ask questions

11. Miko squinted her eyes and studied the map.

12. She marked the map and walked toward the bus stop.

13. A woman stopped and asked Miko a question.

14. Miko understood the question but didn't know the answer.

15. The young girl and woman laughed and shook hands.

16. Miko hurried to the bus stop and boarded the bus.

17. The girl stepped off the bus and crossed the street.

18. The museum was quite large and seemed very busy.

19. The line was long but moved quickly.

20. Miko bought a catalog and read about each painting.

ADDITIONAL PRACTICE
Simple and Compound Sentences

A. Identify each sentence as a *simple sentence* or a *compound sentence.*

Example:

Yoshi and John both play on the basketball team.
simple sentence

1. Yoshi takes ballet lessons.

2. Ballet looks easy but is difficult.

3. John teased Yoshi, and Yoshi didn't like it.

4. Yoshi felt bad but didn't want to admit it.

5. Somehow he must find a solution to the problem.

6. He got a wonderful idea one day.

7. Yoshi asked John to his ballet class as a guest.

8. John refused, but Yoshi insisted.

9. Yoshi took John to class, and John had his first lesson.

10. The exercises were hard, and John couldn't do them.

11. Yoshi had great strength.

12. John's legs were weak.

13. The jumps took strength, and Yoshi jumped higher than anyone else.

14. John was surprised at Yoshi's abilities and apologized to him for his unkind remarks.

Writing Application Collect ideas and images for a poem about dancing. Use at least two compound sentences in your poem.

B. Write each compound sentence. Draw a line under each simple sentence.

Example:

Art of any kind requires devotion, and artists must work hard.

Art of any kind requires devotion, *and artists must work hard*.

15. Dancing requires physical strength, and dancers sometimes have injuries.

16. Athletes often play with injuries, but dancers often have to perform with injuries, too.

17. Artists suffer in other ways, too, and pain is only one kind of hardship.

18. Dancers must pay for lessons, or they must win a scholarship.

19. Many dancers must work to earn money, but this work deprives them of practice time.

20. Being a dancer is often a sacrifice, but it is worth it.

ADDITIONAL PRACTICE

Nouns, Common Nouns, and Proper Nouns

A. Write whether each underlined word names a person, a place, a thing, or an idea.

Example:

The <u>farmer</u> looked at his <u>field</u>.
farmer (person); field (place)

1. The chicken scratched for <u>food</u>.
2. The <u>ground</u> was very dry.
3. Water was scarce on our <u>farm</u>.
4. Our <u>neighbor</u> had to buy <u>water</u> for the <u>cattle</u>.
5. His <u>family</u> had great <u>courage</u>.

B. Read each sentence and write the common nouns.

Example:

The athlete was preparing for the race.
athlete; race

6. Susan swam her last lap in the pool.
7. She was practicing for the competition.
8. Raven was also competing for a medal.
9. She is a runner, not a swimmer.
10. The girls work out each day.

C. Read each sentence and write the proper nouns.

Example:

My cousin Andrea just got back from hiking in the White Mountains.

Andrea; White Mountains

11. These mountains are in northern New Hampshire.

12. Mount Washington, in the White Mountains, is the highest point in New England.

13. Andrea and her friends Mike and Miriam went up to Mount Chocorua.

14. They drove there from Lawrence, Massachusetts.

15. They went hiking along the Kancamagus Highway.

D. Write each proper noun and capitalize it correctly.

16. The lincoln memorial is very beautiful.

17. The white house is located on pennsylvania avenue.

18. While in washington, d.c., we saw a copy of the declaration of independence.

19. uncle ralph visited the house of representatives.

20. aunt margaret spoke with senator dianne feinstein.

ADDITIONAL PRACTICE

Singular and Plural Nouns

A. Read each sentence and write the singular nouns.

Example:

The woman dug up the dry, hard soil.
woman; soil

1. She planted the rosebush carefully.
2. Then she covered the roots with fresh dirt.
3. The garden was her favorite place.
4. From the porch, the woman could see a deer grazing.
5. Without enough rain, the plants would wither.

B. Read each sentence and write the plural nouns.

Example:

The recipe called for six potatoes.
potatoes

6. Two chefs chopped onions.
7. Fresh tomatoes and cucumbers lay on the table.
8. Slices of hot bread were put into baskets.
9. The stew cooked for more than two hours.
10. The vegetables turned to mush.

Writing Application Describe the produce section of a grocery store. Check that you have spelled plural nouns correctly.

C. Proofread each sentence. Decide whether each underlined noun is used correctly or incorrectly. Rewrite each incorrect noun in the correct form.

Example:

Fall is a beautiful <u>seasons</u> of the year.
season

11. The <u>branch</u> of the trees begin to grow bare.
12. The <u>leaf</u> turn yellow and red.
13. The <u>days</u> are noticeably cooler.
14. Animals grow thick <u>coat</u> of hair.
15. <u>Squirrel</u> busily hunt for nuts.
16. You can find <u>jug</u> of fresh cider on the <u>shelves</u> of stores.
17. A frosty <u>morning</u> is a good time to have a <u>bowls</u> of hot oatmeal.
18. Many people travel to farms to pick <u>apple</u> and <u>pear</u>.
19. They put the fruit in <u>basket</u>.
20. A juicy apple is my favorite <u>snacks</u>.
21. Too little rain is not good for apple <u>trees</u>.
22. Too much <u>rainfalls</u> is bad for many <u>crop</u>.
23. Hot sunny days produce healthy <u>ear</u> of <u>corns</u>.
24. <u>Tornado</u> can destroy crops and farmland.
25. <u>Autumns</u> can be a <u>times</u> of rich or poor harvest.

ADDITIONAL PRACTICE

Possessive Nouns

A. Write the singular possessive form of each noun.

Example:

the parent
the parent's

1. the cow
2. the painter
3. the earth
4. the adult
5. Jupiter

6. Charles
7. the child
8. Trish
9. the orchestra
10. the worker

B. Write the plural possessive form of each noun.

Example:

the babies
the babies'

11. the women
12. the farmers
13. the dentists
14. the children
15. the gardeners

16. the sheep
17. the cubs
18. the troops
19. the principals
20. the porpoises

Writing Application Write a narrative telling about an event you remember well. Use two singular and two plural possessive nouns. Share your narrative.

C. Write whether the underlined possessive noun is singular or plural in form.

Example:

The sea <u>cadets'</u> lockers were cleaned.
plural possessive

21. The <u>captain's</u> order was obeyed.

22. The <u>sailors'</u> task was difficult.

23. The <u>seamen's</u> hands tugged at the anchor.

24. The winds blew more fiercely against the <u>vessel's</u> sails.

25. No one had seen the <u>sun's</u> rays for three days.

26. The <u>ship's</u> doctor himself was sick.

27. He worked on to save his <u>companions'</u> lives.

28. Across the water came the sound of <u>people's</u> shouts.

29. The <u>whalers'</u> hearts were lifted.

30. In two <u>months'</u> time, the storm would be only a memory.

ADDITIONAL PRACTICE

Pronouns and Antecedents

A. Write the pronoun or pronouns in each sentence.

Example:

Roger looked at the flute he had just bought.
he

1. Roger said he was going to learn to play the flute.
2. Roger's sister Beth said she also wanted to play in the orchestra.
3. Roger's teacher said, "You must learn the fingering well."
4. She asked him to learn a new piece.
5. The music was difficult, and Roger practiced it for a long time.
6. Beth said she wanted to study the same piece of music.
7. Roger and Beth were nervous when they auditioned for the conductor.
8. She asked Roger to play the piece he had learned, and then she asked Beth to play it.
9. When they got home, Roger and Beth's parents had news for them.
10. They said, "Congratulations, Roger and Beth. You passed the audition."

B. Write the pronoun or pronouns in each sentence. Then write the antecedent of the pronoun.

Example:

In 1843 many people caught what they called "Oregon fever."
they—many people

11. The pioneers traveled along a route they called the Oregon Trail.

12. The trail was about 2,000 miles long, and it followed the Platte River.

13. The travelers followed the trail as they rode west.

14. The trail began in Missouri, and it crossed the Rocky Mountains.

15. One group had almost 1,000 people, and they rode in more than 120 wagons.

16. A special guide was hired, and he planned the details of the trip.

17. The pioneers took along 5,000 farm animals and used them for food.

18. Wagons traveled in a special order, and it never changed.

19. There might be night attacks, so drivers formed wagons into a circle to guard against them.

20. The pioneers crossed a river by fording it, driving the wagons and horses right into it at a shallow point.

ADDITIONAL PRACTICE
Subject Pronouns

A. Write the subject pronoun in each sentence.

Example:

We always learn something useful from Grandmother.
We

1. Yesterday I learned something new about cooking from Grandmother.

2. Before boiling potatoes, she cuts off a slice from the seed end.

3. You may wonder which is the seed end of a potato.

4. Well, it is the end not attached to the vine.

5. It becomes watery in the spring.

6. Potatoes may have watery ends, and then they get bruised.

7. I learned something else.

8. After potatoes are boiled, they should be left to steam in the pot for a while.

9. Grandmother says she uses potatoes to make shortcakes and puddings.

10. She saves on flour and uses less shortening.

Writing Application Write a letter to a friend or relative. List the subject pronouns you use. Then write the noun that each subject pronoun replaces.

B. Write the complete form of the underlined contraction in each sentence.

Example:

Guess where <u>we're</u> going!
we are

11. <u>We're</u> going to the historical museum on Saturday.

12. <u>You'll</u> enjoy the exhibit, too.

13. <u>It's</u> a display of old buggies and carriages.

14. <u>They're</u> examples of how people traveled in the 1800s.

15. <u>I'll</u> get you a ticket.

16. <u>We're</u> leaving early in the morning.

17. <u>You'll</u> even see a Conestoga wagon.

18. <u>I'll</u> bet riding in one was bumpy.

19. <u>I'm</u> sure the roads were unpaved.

20. <u>You'd</u> surely get wet in an open carriage in the rain.

ADDITIONAL PRACTICE

Object Pronouns

C. Write the object pronoun in each sentence.

Example:

Some early laws that applied to horseless carriages might surprise you.
you

21. For example, the Red Flag Law in England in 1865 will amuse you.

22. Drivers of cars had to have a person walking ahead of them waving a red flag.

23. At night the person walking had to carry a red lantern with him.

24. The red objects helped folks on foot by warning them of the car.

25. The driver of the car could drive it no faster than four miles per hour.

26. Believe it or not, that speed was the legal limit until 1896!

27. Speeds gradually rose, so that by 1886 inventors had pushed them up to ten miles per hour.

28. Henry Ford's first automobile plant had only fifty people working in it.

29. The Model T and the Model A were two very popular cars, and Ford's company produced them.

30. The favorite was the Model T; people called it the "Tin Lizzie."

Reflexive Pronouns

D. Write the reflexive pronoun in each sentence.

Example:

Before television, people amused themselves by listening to radio.
themselves

31. At night a family would gather itself around a large radio.

32. Family members sat themselves down in chairs to listen.

33. Every household prided itself on its radio.

34. Stars of vaudeville changed themselves into radio comedians.

35. The first soap operas supported themselves by advertising laundry soap.

36. A radio audience had to imagine for itself the setting and action of the drama.

37. The sound effects booth was in itself a world of wonders.

38. Empty coconut shells could turn themselves into the sounds of horses' hooves.

39. To give the effects of fire, you got yourself some cellophane and crinkled it up.

40. I made myself a list of programs popular in the 1930s and the 1940s.

ADDITIONAL PRACTICE
Possessive Pronouns

A. Write the possessive pronoun in each sentence.

Example:

My aunt and uncle have lots of antiques.
My

1. They store the objects in their house and garage.

2. Aunt Ella owns an antique store near our house.

3. She has had her business for more than ten years.

4. She and Uncle Burt drive their large van to auctions.

5. His favorite antiques are unusual household objects from the nineteenth century.

6. Her collection includes old iceboxes and odd kitchen gadgets.

7. One of my favorites is a device for taking the pits out of cherries.

8. Father said his favorite was a machine for juicing carrots.

9. You might think that people drank the carrot juice for their health.

10. The carrot juice was used to color their homemade butter.

Writing Application Interview an older family member about his or her hobbies. Then write a news story about the hobby. Check to be sure that you have used possessive pronouns correctly.

B. Write the possessive pronoun or pronouns in each sentence. Write whether the pronoun comes *before a noun* or *stands alone*.

Example:

My monthly bill is larger than hers.
My—before a noun; hers—stands alone

11. The credit card originated because people drove their cars everywhere.

12. Every gasoline company wanted its customers to buy its brand of gas.

13. Customers could use their credit cards at gas stations nationwide.

14. The first general cards were issued for eating your dinner at a restaurant.

15. Today Dad has his credit cards.

16. Mother has hers, too.

17. Students in college often have theirs.

18. Your credit card has your picture on it.

19. Mine doesn't.

20. Yours has a special design, but hers is plain.

ADDITIONAL PRACTICE
Adjectives

A. Write the adjectives and articles in each sentence.

Example:

Two stoves sat in the kitchen.
Two; the

1. Grandmother did the weekly washing on the coal-burning stove.

2. Washing was hard work for everyone.

3. Water was heated in big tubs on the stove.

4. Then the dirty clothes were put into the hot water.

5. Grandmother stirred the clothes with a wooden stick.

6. The soapy clothes were then moved to a second tub for rinsing.

7. The rinsed clothes were put through an old-fashioned wringer.

8. Two cylindrical wringers were pressed together as they turned.

9. The wooden wringers were turned by a crank.

10. Finally the clean clothes were taken out and hung on a clothesline.

Writing Application Think of a person you know and like. Make a web of adjectives that describe that person. Then write a sketch of the person.

B. Identify the proper adjectives in each sentence. Then write the proper noun from which each is formed.

Example:

The earliest American immigrants were English people.
American (America); English (England)

11. Other European settlers came soon after.

12. From the seventeenth century to the nineteenth century, few immigrants came to American shores.

13. Asian immigrants helped build America in the 1900s.

14. Chinese immigrants labored to build the railroads.

15. Swedish settlers farmed the plains.

16. Many people have Scandinavian ancestors.

17. German immigrants began farms in Wisconsin and Minnesota.

18. Italian people came to America in the late nineteenth century.

19. Along with Irish immigrants, they settled in the large cities of the East.

20. Spanish people were early settlers of what is now California.

ADDITIONAL PRACTICE
Comparing with Adjectives

A. Complete each sentence by writing the correct form of the adjective in parentheses ( ).

Example:

The first skyscraper in New York was also the (high) building in the world.
highest

1. The (old) building materials were wood and stone.

2. The use of iron and steel made it possible to build (tall) buildings than ever before.

3. The (mighty) advance in the building of skyscrapers was the elevator.

4. Climbing stairs is a (hard) way to get to the top of a building than riding in an elevator.

5. The (early) skyscraper was a twelve-story building in Chicago.

6. By 1889 the world's (high) structure was the Eiffel Tower in Paris.

7. The ground in Chicago is not the (firm) type of soil for tall buildings.

8. The soil there is (loose) and (wet) than it is in New York.

9. In New York, much of the island of Manhattan is composed of rock, the (strong) foundation possible.

10. The Empire State Building, at a height of 1,250 feet, was the (high) skyscraper of its time.

B. Write *more* or *most* to complete the comparison in each sentence.

Example:

Before the railroad, the ____ useful form of transportation was by waterway.
most

11. In Great Britain, the ____ important use for canals was carrying coal.

12. Perhaps the ____ unusual canal of all flowed directly into the coal mines.

13. Carrying coal was ____ expensive before canals were built.

14. Canals soon crisscrossed England, making many businesses ____ profitable than ever.

15. It was ____ difficult for horses to pull loads over muddy roads than along canals.

16. On land the ____ sizable load a horse could pull was about 250 pounds.

17. On a canal, the same horse could pull loads up to 240 times ____ massive than that.

18. The ____ ambitious canals required the building of many locks.

19. Using the locks, boats went from low places to locations that were ____ elevated, and vice versa.

20. The ____ challenging task was to raise or lower the water level.

ADDITIONAL PRACTICE

Comparing with Adjectives

21. The technique used was ____ complicated than you might think.

22. The ____ mysterious part of canal building is how locks were developed.

23. The ____ ancient drawings of locks were made by Leonardo da Vinci.

24. One of the ____ puzzling questions involves how locks open.

25. To the Italians, opening lock gates vertically seemed ____ efficient than opening them horizontally.

26. Belgium has some of the ____ ancient canals in the world.

27. The Erie Canal in New York is ____ recent than canals in many parts of Europe.

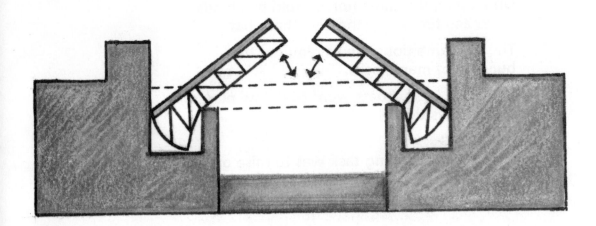

C. Complete each sentence by writing the correct form of the adjective shown in parentheses ( ).

Example:

To go short distances, railroads are (good) than airplanes or automobiles.
better

28. The speed of trains is (good) than ever before.

29. The (good) thing of all about trains is that you can travel from the center of one city to the center of another.

30. My grandfather said taking the Interurban from Urbana, Illinois, to Decatur, Illinois, was (good) than driving.

31. He said that the (good) reason to have those trains was that they connected all the midsize cities in Illinois.

32. In some ways, rail travel is (good) than it used to be.

33. In other ways, it is (bad).

34. Grandfather thinks rail travel will be (good) than ever because of new high-speed trains.

35. Travel conditions on early railroads were far (bad) than they are today.

36. The (bad) thing of all about early trains was the thick smoke that poured out of the engines.

37. I can't imagine anything (good) than traveling from Los Angeles to San Francisco in less than three hours.

ADDITIONAL PRACTICE

Verbs

A. Identify the verb used in each sentence.

Example:

Our house has a large fireplace.
has

1. Another name for a fireplace is a hearth.
2. Hearths provided heat for the living room.
3. No one strayed far from the fireplace in winter.
4. Fireplaces often had two or three hooks.
5. Each hook swung away from the fire.

B. Identify the action verb used in each sentence.

Example:

I found these books in the attic.
found

6. This diary contains a lot of our family history.
7. It tells a fascinating story.
8. Our ancestors traveled a long way.
9. They settled in the Middle West.
10. That trunk holds photographs from the old days.
11. Old photographs fade.
12. Grandfather took many pictures of his bride-to-be.

13. **This picture shows my grandmother in a bathing suit.**

14. **These bathing suits covered one's entire body.**

15. **Women wore bathing hats as well.**

C. Identify the linking verb in each sentence.

Example:

That woman looks familiar.
looks

16. **Yes, she is my grandmother.**

17. **She is also the woman in this photograph.**

18. **The occasion was a Fourth of July picnic.**

19. **Family reunions became a tradition.**

20. **Our family remains close.**

21. **That tree in the background was only an acorn in 1888.**

22. **It became a huge oak tree.**

23. **This photo of the tree is my favorite.**

24. **The tree seems young and sturdy.**

25. **It is healthy even today.**

Writing Application Think about two things that are both alike and different. Organize your ideas in a Venn diagram. Then write a comparison and contrast essay. Use at least five linking verbs in your essay.

ADDITIONAL PRACTICE

Main Verbs and Helping Verbs

A. Write the main verb used in each sentence.

Example:

In July you can see lots of fireflies.
see

1. July has always reminded me of fireflies.
2. You can see them every evening then.
3. I have always connected them with the Fourth of July.
4. We would watch the fireworks then.
5. Between the displays, the fireflies would dance.
6. Fireflies are also called *lightning bugs.*
7. A firefly can be considered a beetle.
8. Fireflies have always seemed like little UFOs to me.
9. You will spot them in one place.
10. Then suddenly they will have moved to another place.

Writing Application Imagine you are an insect. Tell what you observe. Find the helping verbs and main verbs in your sentences. Share your description.

B. Write the helping verb and the main verb used in each sentence.

Example:

The circus will always be my favorite entertainment.
will; be

11. Do you see that little car?

12. A clown is driving it.

13. The car is coming toward us.

14. It has stopped right in front of us.

15. The door has opened.

16. The clown is stepping out of the car.

17. What did you say?

18. I have counted four clowns so far.

19. Eight clowns have emerged from that little car.

20. How do they squeeze into that small space?

21. No one would believe it.

22. Do you see a hole in the ground anywhere?

23. Can more clowns be in there?

24. I have not counted twelve clowns.

25. How can twelve clowns fit in a car so small!

Practice

ADDITIONAL PRACTICE

Tense

A. Write whether the verb used in each sentence is in the *present tense*, the *past tense*, or the *future tense*.

Example:

I stand in front of the audience.
stand — present tense

1. The play will be next week.
2. I have the leading role.
3. We rehearsed for four weeks.
4. I memorized all my lines.
5. My best friend helped me.
6. I will tell you the story of the play.
7. No one believes me.
8. I come from another planet.
9. I wear green makeup.
10. You will be surprised!

Writing Application Choose three articles from your local newspaper: one written in present tense, one in past tense, and one in future tense. Choose one article, and write a summary of it in the same tense used in the article.

Present Tense

B. Complete each sentence correctly by writing the present-tense form of the verb shown in parentheses ( ).

Example:

Art (be) my hobby.
is

11. I (begin) art classes today.
12. My teacher (be) Mr. Nunez.
13. I (have) all my equipment.
14. The class (meet) in a large studio.
15. My sister Lise (paint) well.
16. She (observe) objects very carefully.
17. Now I (notice) things differently, too.
18. I (be) aware of details.
19. This shade of blue (look) right.
20. Strong colors often (go) well together.
21. Mr. Nunez (teach) three classes.
22. Lise and I (be) in two of them.
23. Lise (sketch) like a professional.
24. Her sense of humor (show) here.
25. (Be) this a drawing of you?

ADDITIONAL PRACTICE

Past Tense

A. Complete each sentence correctly by writing the past-tense form of the verb shown in parentheses ( ).

Example:

We (park) our car in the lot.
parked

1. Many people (wait) in line.
2. The water (look) cool.
3. Lifeguards (watch) the swimmers.
4. The toddlers (play) in shallow water.
5. Their mothers (watch) them carefully.
6. I (enjoy) my swimming lessons last year.
7. The slide (end) in the water.
8. I (climb) up the ladder.
9. The water (moisten) the surface of the slide.
10. The water (cool) me.
11. The person before me (splash) in the water.
12. She (paddle) in the waves.
13. I (reach) for the edges of the slide.
14. I (push) myself off down the slide.
15. Before long, I (plop) into the pool.

16. My mother and sister (laugh) at me.

17. Our dog Rusty (bark) at me noisily.

18. Then my sister and I (join) a water polo game.

19. She (place) me on her shoulders.

20. Soon I (tumble) off into the water.

21. By noontime, we all (want) food.

22. We (unpack) our picnic basket under the trees.

23. Rusty (wag) his tail eagerly.

24. The food (taste) good.

25. Our day at the pool (end) before sundown.

Writing Application Write a narrative about something you did during the summer. Use past–tense verbs.

ADDITIONAL PRACTICE

Irregular Verbs

A. Complete each sentence correctly by writing the present-tense form of the verb shown in parentheses ( ).

Example:

Our school (have) a music club.
has

1. Robin (bring) her guitar to our weekly meetings.

2. She (be) our accompanist.

3. We (sing) songs at each meeting.

4. Robin (do) very well on the guitar.

5. Hers (be) an acoustic guitar.

6. Our teacher, Mrs. Melendez, (make) us rehearse frequently.

7. She (know) music very well.

8. At each meeting she (give) us harmony lessons.

9. Tonight we (begin) practicing for a concert.

10. Robin (write) original music for us.

11. Music (make) me happy.

12. (Be) you a singer?

13. Most of our songs (be) in three parts.

14. Three-part music (be) difficult.

15. Alexa usually (take) the alto part.

16. Sally (have) a higher voice.

17. Sally and four others (sing) first soprano.

18. Our chorus (do) very well with so few singers.

19. We are excited when we (give) our first concert of the year.

20. Alexa (do) our posters.

21. This one from last year (be) my favorite.

22. It (have) four colors.

23. The musical notes (begin) an old song.

24. My mother (know) all the words.

25. The first part of the song (go) like this.

26. Val always (eat) something before singing.

27. Everyone usually (drink) something during rehearsals.

28. Who (have) an extra ticket for the concert?

29. Sally (do).

30. There (be) no more empty seats.

Writing Application Imagine that you are performing in a concert at your school. Write a narrative in the present tense about what you do, see, hear, and feel. Use several irregular verbs.

Practice

ADDITIONAL PRACTICE

Irregular Verbs

B. Complete each sentence correctly by writing the past-tense form of the irregular verb shown in parentheses ( ).

Example:

Our family (go) to an amusement park last week.
went

31. The fun house (be) our first stop.

32. I (see) myself in the funny mirrors.

33. Then we (ride) in a little train through a long tunnel.

34. I (be) scared of the horrible sights.

35. Dad (bring) a camera.

36. He (take) pictures of some of the eerie creatures.

37. The train (make) a sharp turn.

38. It almost (run) off the tracks.

39. I (think) I would faint.

40. The experience (give) me goose bumps.

41. After that, we (have) lunch.

42. At first, I (eat) nothing.

43. I (be) hungry though.

44. We (bring) a picnic lunch.

45. By two o'clock, the sky (grow) cloudy.

46. Next (come) the rides.

47. My brother (see) the roller coaster.

48. Dad (give) the ticket seller money for the ride.

49. I (run) to the last two cars.

50. I (ride) in the last car.

51. From the top, we (see) the whole park.

52. The first drop (be) the steepest one.

53. The passengers (make) a lot of noise.

54. The whole trip (take) almost five minutes.

55. We (go) on the roller coaster two more times.

56. After that, we (come) to the Ferris wheel.

57. Dad (take) us all on that ride, too.

58. The wheel (do) a funny thing.

59. When we were at the top, it (come) to a stop.

60. That real incident (be) scarier than the silly things in the fun house.

ADDITIONAL PRACTICE

Future Tense

A. Write the future-tense form of the verb shown in parentheses ( ) to complete each sentence.

Example:

School (begin) in two weeks.
will begin

1. I (be) in the fifth grade then.
2. My sister Andrea and I (attend) a new school.
3. A bus (take) us there.
4. Many of my friends (go) with us.
5. Andrea (be) in the sixth grade.
6. This (be) Andrea's second year at that school.
7. We both (have) new teachers.
8. Her former teacher (be) my new one.
9. In October, auditions (begin) for Student Night.
10. I (try) for a part in the show.

11. Andrea (sing) two numbers.

12. Our parents (come) to the opening performance.

13. Other relatives (arrive) just in time for the final performance.

14. My cousin and I (open) the show.

15. We (do) a tap dance.

16. We (wear) tap shoes and flashy suits.

17. In all, forty students (perform).

18. The show (raise) money for the art and music departments.

19. Some of that money (go) for new instruments.

20. This year Andrea (study) the clarinet.

Writing Application What kinds of transportation will people use 100 years from now? Write about your predictions, using the future tense. Remember to provide reasons and details.

ADDITIONAL PRACTICE

Adverbs

A. For each sentence, write the adverb that describes each underlined word. Then write whether the adverb tells *how, when, where,* or *to what extent.*

Example:

Our dog Sasha is a very <u>loving</u> pet.
very; to what extent

1. Sasha <u>lay</u> quietly on the rug.

2. She <u>slept</u> there in the afternoon.

3. She suddenly <u>lifted</u> her head.

4. She <u>rose</u> quickly from her spot.

5. She <u>went</u> to the door anxiously.

6. I soon <u>heard</u> a knock at the door.

7. Josepha, our mail carrier, pleasantly <u>surprised</u> us with a package.

8. Sasha <u>greeted</u> her noisily.

9. The happy dog <u>stood</u> there wagging her tail.

10. Josepha <u>scratched</u> Sasha lovingly under the chin.

11. Sasha always <u>hears</u> every sound.

12. Sounds often <u>wake</u> her from sleep.

13. She regularly <u>announces</u> visitors.

14. She is very <u>happy</u> to see our friends.

15. She is extremely <u>cautious</u> with strangers.

16. Sasha once <u>had</u> an accident.

17. She nearly <u>lost</u> her life.

18. The vet <u>acted</u> quickly.

19. He <u>removed</u> one hind leg completely.

20. Now Sasha <u>walks</u> on three legs.

21. She soon <u>became</u> an expert at "hop-walking."

22. In spite of the loss, she moves quite <u>efficiently</u>.

23. Her disposition is extremely <u>pleasant</u>.

24. After school she <u>waits</u> patiently for me at the door.

25. I arrive and she <u>jumps</u> up.

26. I <u>stoop</u> down for her.

27. I always <u>bring</u> something for her.

28. She is very <u>faithful</u> to us.

29. Hop-walking sometimes <u>tires</u> her.

30. She <u>flops</u> down on the rug to rest.

ADDITIONAL PRACTICE

Comparing with Adverbs

A. Write the form of the adverb shown in parentheses ( ) that correctly completes each sentence.

Example:

This plant blooms (late) than that one.
later

1. Plants grow (fast) with fertilizer than they do without fertilizer.

2. Dig this hole (deep) into the ground than the last one.

3. Make it (wide) than you did before.

4. In this country, spring comes (early) of all in the South.

5. Plants suffer from frost (hard) of all in the northern states.

6. Can you stand (close) than that to this sapling?

7. You must grasp the trunk (high) than this, or the tree will fall.

8. We planted saplings (late) than usual this year.

9. This year's crop will mature (soon) than last year's.

10. The wet weather lasted (long) than usual.

B. Write the form of the adverb shown in parentheses ( ) that correctly completes each sentence.

Example:

Forecasters can predict weather (accurately) than before.
more accurately

11. A car can skid (quickly) on icy streets than on rainy streets.

12. Radio newscasts provide weather updates (regularly) than do TV reports.

13. Weather forecasts can change (surprisingly) of all when wind patterns change.

14. Some parts of the nation get large amounts of rain (often) than others.

15. Forecasters can predict (accurately) of all in places where conditions change slowly.

C. Complete each sentence with the form of *well* or *badly* that makes sense.

Example:

Do large solar panels work (well) than small ones?
better

16. Solar panels work (well) of all with lots of sunshine.

17. They operate (bad) of all in cloudy conditions.

18. I think I like solar panels (well) than windmills.

19. Geothermal energy may do (well) than either wind or solar power.

ADDITIONAL PRACTICE
Negatives

A. Write the word shown in parentheses ( ) that correctly completes each sentence. Avoid double negatives.

Example:

Not many people (have, haven't) seen a forest fire.
have

1. A forest fire isn't (never, ever) the end of a forest.

2. The little trees and bushes can't (ever, never) get much sunshine in an old forest.

3. The biggest trees don't (never, ever) let the sunshine in.

4. If the big trees don't die or burn, the little saplings can't (ever, never) grow.

5. No fire (never, ever) starts without a cause.

6. There doesn't have to be (no, any) human cause for a fire.

7. Haven't you (never, ever) heard of lightning causing a fire?

8. Not (everyone, no one) remembers that.

9. Didn't (nobody, anybody) show you pictures of Mount St. Helens after the eruption?

10. I haven't (never, ever) seen so many trees burned.

11. The damage wasn't caused by (no, any) forest fire.

12. I didn't have (any, no) idea that lava could be so destructive.

13. You couldn't imagine (anything, nothing) more surprising than that volcano now.

14. There's not (no, any) ground that's still barren.

15. Why didn't (no one, anyone) show us those pictures until now?

16. Aren't there (no, any) pictures of Yellowstone National Park?

17. Didn't (nobody, anybody) tell you about the fire there?

18. After the fire, animals couldn't find (any, no) grass to eat.

19. There (was, wasn't) no vegetation where the fire had burned.

20. Fortunately, it didn't take (any, no) time for new grass began to sprout.

Writing Application Write a silly story about a day when nothing happens normally. Use negatives such as *no, none* and *nobody* in your story. Read your story aloud to classmates.

ADDITIONAL PRACTICE

Prepositions and Prepositional Phrases

A. Identify the preposition used in each sentence.

Example:

Do you know about the Endangered Species Act?
about

1.   Some species couldn't survive without it.
2.   Have you ever seen a falcon in flight?
3.   The falcon almost became extinct from DDT poisoning.
4.   The peregrine falcon is loved for its graceful flight.
5.   It can dive at great speeds.

B. The object of the preposition in each sentence is underlined. Write the preposition for each object.

Example:

Fifteen inches is the length of an average <u>falcon</u>.
of

6.   Have you ever seen a falcon dive toward the <u>earth</u>?
7.   A peregrine falcon has a wingspan of forty <u>inches</u>.
8.   In the <u>1970s</u> there were fewer than 2,000 falcons.
9.   The effect of <u>DDT</u> prevented falcon reproduction.
10.   The falcon population has increased by eight <u>thousand</u>.

11. The increase in <u>numbers</u> is quite impressive.

12. The U.S. Fish and Wildlife Service may remove the species from its endangered <u>list</u>.

13. Falcons can even be seen on <u>Golden Gate Bridge</u>.

14. I have seen them also in <u>Boston</u>.

15. They have adapted well to these unusual <u>homes</u>.

C. Write the prepositional phrase used in each sentence. Underline the preposition.

Example:

Trainers of falcons are called *falconers*.
<u>of</u> falcons

16. Training them takes a good deal of time.

17. The birds must often wear hoods over their heads.

18. The falcon flies away into the sky.

19. Then it must return to its trainer.

20. Falcons are prized for their hunting ability.

21. Some people do not like birds of prey.

22. They do not realize the importance of natural predators.

23. Keeping animal populations in balance is important.

24. Preying birds, or raptors, help in this process.

25. Every creature has an important place in nature.

ADDITIONAL PRACTICE

Troublesome Words

A. Write the word in parentheses ( ) that correctly completes each sentence.

Example:

I have not been performing (good, well) lately.
well

1. This chicken soup tastes (good, well).

2. Many more than just (too, to, two) folk remedies for colds are known.

3. I suppose (there, they're, their) is some good in them all.

4. Some say chicken soup will make you (good, well).

5. Experts say (its, it's) the selenium in the soup.

6. This element is a (good, well) substance to take for a cold.

7. (Their, There, They're) is another helpful thing to do when you are sick.

8. Doctors say that drinking fluids is a (well, good) thing for a cold.

9. (Your, You're) never wrong to do that.

10. Drinking fluids is (well, good) for you most of the time.

11. (To, Too, Two) me, fluids are enough to cure a cold.

12. But (there, their, they're) are still more remedies.

13. Grandmother would always plaster (your, you're) chest with a mustard plaster.

14. It was supposed to make you (good, well) overnight.

15. It certainly smelled awful (to, two, too) me.

16. Did your grandmother do that, (to, too, two)?

17. (You're, Your) not joking, are you?

18. (Its, It's) no coincidence, I guess.

19. A lot of people used home remedies to help themselves get (good, well).

20. Rest is also an important part of (your, you're) recovery.

21. (Its, It's) no fun lying in bed.

22. Sleep can help make you (good, well).

23. Isn't laughter also (good, well) for you?

24. Yes, laughter is (you're, your) best friend.

25. Laughing is something I do (well, good).

ADDITIONAL PRACTICE

Troublesome Words

B. Write the word in parentheses ( ) that correctly completes each sentence.

Example:

A proper diet should play (its, it's) part in (good, well) health.

its; good

26. Food that is (well, good) for you should taste (good, well), too.

27. That's not (to, too, two) much (to, too, two) ask, is it?

28. (Its, It's) not easy (to, too, two) eat food that tastes terrible.

29. If food doesn't taste (good, well), it doesn't matter whether (there, their, they're) is great nutrition in it.

30. I'm glad (your, you're) in agreement with that.

31. Do you see that restaurant down (their, they're, there)?

32. (Its, It's) a popular restaurant with (good, well) chefs.

33. I think (their, they're, there) secret is (well, good) seasoning.

34. (They're, Their, There) always busy down (their, they're, there) in the restaurant.

35. I think (your, you're) wallet could take it.

36. Would you like to eat (their, there, they're) sometime?

37. "(Good, Well) food (good, well) prepared" is (their, they're, there) motto.

38. (Its, It's) a goal of mine (to, too, two) run a restaurant.

39. The (to, too, two) of us would make a great team.

40. My uncle says (your, you're) never (to, two, too) young to plan such a thing.

41. He says (they're, their, there) is always room for a good restaurant.

42. I myself think (their, there, they're) are (to, two, too) many bad restaurants around.

43. You shouldn't serve people (two, to, too) much food.

44. Less is more when it comes (to, too, two) (well, good) cooking.

45. (Two, To, Too) much food can be bad for (your, you're) health.

ADDITIONAL PRACTICE
Punctuation: Comma

A. Write each sentence, adding commas where they are needed.

Example:

The three planets farthest from the sun are Uranus Neptune and Pluto.
The three planets farthest from the sun are Uranus, Neptune, and Pluto.

1. Yes each of the planets rotates on an axis.

2. Lucy name the planet nearest the sun.

3. Yes there are nine planets in all.

4. Oh I believe the two largest planets are Jupiter and Saturn.

5. Well the four planets nearest the sun are called terrestrial planets.

6. They are Mercury Venus Earth and Mars.

7. Yes the atmospheres of these planets contain mostly nitrogen and carbon dioxide.

8. No John the other planets have atmospheres made up mostly of four other gases.

9. Those four gases are helium hydrogen methane and ammonia.

10. Yes Marcia Earth is the only planet with a large amount of oxygen.

11. Yes astronomers believe there are planets around other stars in the universe.

12. Did you know Cecilie that there are more than 100 billion stars in our galaxy?

13. Yes the name of our galaxy is the Milky Way.

14. More than 100 billion galaxies can be seen Ned.

15. Yes that is an amazingly large number.

16. Which way do the planets move Penny as we look at them?

17. Yes Penny they move from east to west.

18. The three planets you can see most easily are Venus Jupiter and Saturn.

19. Mercury's year is only 88 days long Ted.

20. Well that's just about one-fourth as long as a year on the planet Earth.

21. Yes the astronomer Ptolemy thought the Earth was the center of the universe.

22. Juan his theory was accepted for more than 1,000 years.

23. Well it was not until 1543 that this view changed.

24. Copernicus was a student of mathematics law and medicine.

25. Ptolemy Copernicus and Kepler were important in early astronomy.

ADDITIONAL PRACTICE
Punctuation: Comma

B. Add a comma to each compound sentence where it is needed. Not all sentences are compound sentences.

Example:

This telescope is strong but that star is quite far away.
This telescope is strong, but that star is quite far away.

26. The astronomy club meets once a month and students go on field trips three times a year.

27. Once we went to an observatory but the telescope could not produce good pictures.

28. Telescopes are aimed at stars but scientists cannot always see the objects in space.

29. There are good observatories in the United States but the light here is too bright.

30. Light from cities can cause problems for scientists and other observers.

31. People in cities need to see at night but street lamps affect telescopes.

32. Some cities use yellow street lights and these lights do not cause problems for telescopes.

33. White street lights interfere with the view and scientists cannot use their telescopes.

34. Dark nights are best for observing stars and other objects in the sky.

35. Astronomers have to wait for good conditions or they must go to distant places.

36. Some scientists travel to Peru to observe the skies.

37. There is light in these places but it is much less bright.

38. Telescopes in the United States are expensive and they stand idle.

39. Some of the best telescopes in the world are here but they cannot be used.

40. Scientists used to drive just a few miles to see the stars but now they must fly hundreds of miles.

41. The nearest stars are visible without telescopes or binoculars.

42. Light from distant stars has traveled far and some stars are millions of light-years away.

43. Light travels about 186,000 miles per second and that is quite an amazing speed.

44. You can multiply to see how many miles it travels in a year but you would need a lot of paper to do your figuring.

45. I tried the problem on my calculator and the figures ran off the screen.

ADDITIONAL PRACTICE

Dialogue

A. Write each sentence. Add quotation marks where they are needed.

Example:

When are you leaving? asked Ron.
"When are you leaving?" asked Ron.

1. We have to be at the airport by 3:00 P.M., replied Flora.

2. It takes time to check in, her mother said.

3. Yes, said Ron's father, you have to go through a metal detector.

4. Before that, said Flora, we have to check our bags.

5. I wish I were going with you, said Ron.

6. You just got back from a trip yourself, said Flora's mother.

7. I know, said Ron. We went to Chicago.

8. The plane was not in the air long, said Ron.

9. Ron's father said, Yes, it took longer to get to the airport than it did to fly to Chicago!

10. In Chicago, Ron added, there is a rapid-transit train that goes downtown from the airport.

11. Flora asked, Did you take the train?

12. Ron's father said, No, we were not going downtown.

13. Our destination was Evanston, Ron explained. My aunt lives there.

14. Did you see any sights while you were there? asked Flora's mother.

15. Oh, we certainly did, said Ron's father.

16. The first day we went to the Brookfield Zoo, said Ron.

17. That zoo is quite large, said Flora's mother.

18. It covers quite a bit of ground, said Ron, like the zoos in San Diego and in the Bronx, New York.

19. The next day we went to the Museum of Science and Industry, said Ron's father.

20. Ron added, That place is so large that you can't see it all in one day.

21. I don't think you're supposed to, laughed Flora's mother.

22. People go back to see different exhibits, I guess, said Ron.

23. Well, said Flora's mother, we must get out to the airport.

24. Bring me back a souvenir, Flora, said Ron.

25. Don't you worry, Ron, replied Flora. I will.

Writing Application Imagine that you and a friend are on a space voyage. Brainstorm ideas for a dialogue you might have. Then write the dialogue, being sure to use quotation marks correctly.

ADDITIONAL PRACTICE

Titles

A. Write the titles used in the following sentences correctly.

Example:

Where is the new copy of the national geographic magazine?
National Geographic

1. It's over there on the table next to newsweek.

2. I want to read the article entitled space shuttles.

3. I think time magazine also has an article about space stations.

4. It's called shuttling around earth.

5. I still remember the movie close encounters of the third kind.

6. I read a poem about space called worlds out there.

7. It's in a book entitled inner and outer space.

8. Did you watch that TV program on nova?

9. Let's watch star trek v tonight.

10. Oh, I forgot and rented indiana jones and the temple of doom.

11. Don is going to watch a rerun of star wars.

12. José wants to finish the puzzle in the New York times.

13. I may bring aunt liz a videocassette of flash gordon.

14. She might like around the world in 80 days.

15. I'll bet dad would like this one called touring america's national parks.

16. Yes, I read an article about it in AAA world.

17. Let's not forget to watch jeopardy tonight.

18. Later we can watch beauty and the beast.

19. Don't you have to finish reading that story, the gift of the magi?

20. I already finished reading that and a poem called chicago by carl sandburg.

Writing Application Draw a cartoon that shows two characters talking about their favorite books or stories. Place the characters' words in speech balloons. Be sure to punctuate the titles correctly. Exchange cartoons with a partner to proofread.

ADDITIONAL PRACTICE

Abbreviations

A. Write the abbreviation of each term. Use a dictionary if you need to.

Example:

Boulevard
Blvd.

1. Alabama
2. Michigan
3. Virginia
4. New Mexico
5. California
6. Texas
7. Massachusetts
8. Connecticut
9. Maine
10. Monday

11. Saturday
12. Tuesday
13. Wednesday
14. 5 inches
15. 12 feet
16. 1,200 meters
17. 2 quarts
18. 4 gallons
19. 5 pounds
20. 14 ounces

21. **President Bush**

22. **Governor Richards**

23. **Reverend Alvin Greene**

24. **Doctor Amy Chang**

25. **Mister James Mendez**

26. **General Omar Bradley**

27. **Captain MacIntosh**

28. **October 13**

29. **January 22**

30. **August 20**

31. **September 13**

32. **Bond Street**

33. **River Road**

34. **Michigan Avenue**

35. **Sunset Drive**

36. **Columbia University**

37. **Washington High School**

38. **United States**

39. **Mount McKinley**

40. **Saint Augustine**

Note: Italic page numbers refer to Additional Practice.

A

Abbreviations, 117–119, *252–253*

Action verbs. *See* **Verbs.**

Additional Practice, *183–253*

abbreviations, *252–253*

adjectives, *212–217*

adverbs, *232–235*

dialogue, *248–249*

negatives, *236–237*

nouns, *198–203*

prepositions, *238–239*

pronouns, *204–211*

punctuation, *244–247*

sentences, *184–197*

titles, *250–251*

usage, *240–243*

verbs, *218–231*

Adjectives, 141–149, *212–217*

that compare, 147–149, *214–217*

Adverbs, 174–179, *232–235*

negatives, 171–173, *236–237*

that compare, 177–179, *234–235*

Apostrophe

in contractions, 171–173

in possessive nouns, 123–125

Articles, 141–143, *212*

B

Book review, 84

Brainstorming for writing ideas, 2, 6–9

C

Capitalization

proper nouns, 117–119, *198–199*

sentences, 93–98, *185*

titles, *250–251*

Case, 135–137

Character sketch, 63

Charts, making, 88–90

Clauses, 111–113

Commas, 111, *244–247*

after introductory words, 111

in compound sentences, 108

in direct address, *248–249*

Common nouns. *See* **Nouns.**

Comparison. *See* **Paragraph.**

Comparisons

using figurative language, 15–17

with adjectives, 147–149, *214–217*

with adverbs, 177–179, *234–235*

Composition. *See* **Writing process.**

Conferencing, 3, 48–49

Conjunction, 108

Contractions, 171

Contrast. *See* **Paragraph.**

Conventions, 34–35

Cross-curricular writing, 74–80, 88–90

Declarative sentence, 93–95, *186–187*

Descriptive writing.
See **Writing forms and models.**

Details, 22–25

Development, 22–25

Diagram, making, 88–90

Dialogue, *248–249*

Direct address, *248–249*

Direct quotations, *248–249*

Directions. *See* **How-to.**

Drafting, 12, 20–21

Drama, 86–87

Editing, 2, 9, 13, 17, 21, 25, 29, 33, 34–35

Editor's marks, 9, 13, 17, 21, 25, 29, 33

Effective paragraphs, 30–33

Effective sentences, 26–29

Elaborating. *See* **Development.**

E-mail, 45

Essay

comparison and contrast, 72–73

descriptive, 61–62

explanation, 74–75

how-to, 71

persuasive, 83

response to literature, 64–65

summary, 66–67

that compares and contrasts, 72–73

Everyday writing, 81, 88–90

Exclamatory sentence, 96–98, *186–187*

Expository writing.
See **Writing forms and models.**

Facts to support opinion, 22–25, 82, 83, 84, 85

Figurative language, 15–17

Final draft, 2, 36–39

Focus/Ideas, 6–9

Folktale, 58

Forms, 81

G

Grammar, 93–182
    See also **Additional Practice**
Graphics, 88–90

H

Handwriting, 40–44
Helping verbs, 150–152, *220–221*
How-to
    essay, 71
    paragraph, 70

I

Ideas for writing, 2–3, 6–9
Imperative sentence, 96–98, *186–187*
Information paragraph, 69
Interrogative sentence, 93–95, *186–187*
Interview, 76
Introductory words, comma with, 111, *244–245*
Irregular verbs, 165–167, *226–229*

L

Linking verbs, 153-155, *218–219*

Listening. *See* **Speaking and listening.**

M

Main verb, 150-152, *220–221*
Mechanics, *244–253*
    See also **Commas, Quotation marks, and Titles.**

N

Naming part of sentence (subject), 99–101, *188–191, 194–195*
    joining naming parts (subjects), 105–107, *194–195*
Narrative writing.
    See **Writing forms and models.**
Narrowing a topic, 7
Negatives, 171–173, *236–237*
News story, 76–77
Note-taking, 78
Nouns, 117–125, *198–203*
    common, 117–119, *198–199*
    plural, 120-122, *200–201*
    possessive, 123–125, *202–203*
    proper, 117–119, *198–199*
    singular, 120–122, *200–201*

O

Object of preposition,
180–182, *238–239*

Object pronoun.
See **Pronouns.**

Opinion, 22–25, 82–83, 84–85

Oral report. *See* **Presentation.**

Organization, 10–13

Outline, 79

P

Paragraph
descriptive, 60
how-to, 70
of information, 69
persuasive, 82

Peer Conferences, 48–49

Period
with abbreviations, 117
with declarative
sentence, 93–95, *186–187*
with imperative
sentence, 96–98, *186–187*

Personal narrative, 68

Persuasive writing,
See **Writing forms
and models.**

Play, 86–87

Plural nouns, 120–122,
200–201

Portfolio, 3

Possessive nouns, 123–125,
202–203

Possessive pronouns, 132–134,
210–211

Practice. *See* **Additional
practice.**

Predicate, 102–107, *188–189*,
192–193
complete, 102–104,
192–193
compound, 105–107,
194–195
simple, 102–104, *192–193*

Preposition. *See* **Object of the
preposition and
Prepositional phrase.**

Prepositional phrase, 180–182,
238–239

Presentation, 36–39

Prompt, responding to a,
8, 12, 16, 20, 24, 28, 32,
52–54

Pronouns, 126–140, *204–211*
antecedent, 126–128,
204–205
object, 129–131, *208*
possessive, 132–134,
210–211
reflexive, 138–140, *209*
subject, 129–131, *206–207*

Proofreading, 2, 9, 13, 17, 21,
25, 29, 33, 34–35

Proper nouns, 117–119,
198–199

U

Usage, *240–243*

V

Venn diagram, 90
Verb tenses, 156–161,
    168–170, *222–231*
    future, 159–161, *230–231*
    past, 159–161, *224–225*
    perfect, 168–170
    present, 156–158, *222–223*
Verbs, 150–170, *218–231*
    action, 153–155, *218–219*
    helping, 150–152, *220–221*
    irregular, 165–167, *226–229*
    linking, 153–155, *218–219*
    main, 150–152, *218–221*
Visuals, 36–39, 88–90
Vivid words, using, 14–17,
    18–21
Voice, 14–17

Word choice, 18–21
Writer's craft, 4–39
Writing for a test, 52–54
Writing forms and models
    book review, 84
    character sketch, 63

charts, making, 88–90
comparison and contrast
    essay, 72–73
descriptive essay, 61–62
descriptive paragraph, 60
diagrams, making, 88–90
essay that explains, 74–75
folktale, 58
forms, 81
how-to essay, 71
how-to paragraph, 70
information, paragraph
    of, 69
news story, 76–77
note-taking skills, 78
personal narrative, 68
persuasive essay, 83
persuasive paragraph, 82
play, 86–87
research report, 78–80
response to literature,
    64–65
story, 56–57
summary, 66–67
tall tale, 59
television/movie review, 85
using charts, graphs, and
    diagrams, 88–90
Writing process, 2, 8–9, 12–13,
    16–17, 20–21, 24–25, 28–29,
    32–33, 34–35, 36–39,
    48–49